LAWRENCE OF ARABIA'S SECRET AIR FORCE

LAWRENCE OF ARABIA'S SECRET AIR FORCE

BASED ON THE DIARY OF FLIGHT SERGEANT GEORGE HYNES

BY

JAMES PATRICK HYNES

First published in Great Britain in 2010 by
Pen & Sword Aviation
An imprint of
Pen & Sword Books Ltd
47 Church Street
Barnsley
South Yorkshire
S70 2AS

Copyright © James Patrick Hynes 2010

ISBN 978 1 84884 266 3

Typeset by Acredula

Printed and bound in England
by the MPG Books Group

Pen & Sword Books Ltd incorporates the Imprints of Pen & Sword Aviation,
Pen & Sword Family History, Pen & Sword Maritime, Pen & Sword Military,
Wharncliffe Local History, Pen & Sword Select, Pen & Sword Military Classics,
Leo Cooper, Remember When, Seaforth Publishing and Frontline Publishing

For a complete list of Pen & Sword titles please contact
PEN & SWORD BOOKS LIMITED
47 Church Street, Barnsley, South Yorkshire, S70 2AS, England
E-mail: enquiries@pen-and-sword.co.uk
Website: www.pen-and-sword.co.uk

Contents

Acknowledgements

I am most grateful to my cousin, Ellen Gannicott (née Hynes), for preserving and making available her father's memoirs.

A Tribute from Lawrence

In a foreword written in Cranwell on 15 August 1926 and signed T.E.S. Lawrence he paid tribute to a number of named persons but there he also wrote:

> And there were many other leaders or lonely fighters to whom this self-regardent picture is not fair. It is still less fair, of course, like all war-stories, to the un-named rank and file who miss their share of credit, as they must do, until they can write the despatches.

Preface

The exploits of Lawrence of Arabia have been well documented in his own books, *Seven Pillars of Wisdom* and *Revolt in the Desert*, for example, and indeed in many of his writings including his prolific correspondence. Among the many surviving letters written by him are two received by my uncle, Number 3064, Flight Sergeant George Samuel Hynes who served with the secret X Flight of the Royal Flying Corps in close support of Lawrence and his Arabs. Air Mechanic G.S. Hynes, of No. 14 Squadron, met and spoke with Lawrence on several occasions. In fact on one occasion he was called upon to repair an aircraft downed in the desert with Lawrence as passenger.

More often than not books about war service have been written by commissioned ranks and/or politicians but the memoirs presented in this book have been written by a ranker whose skills, along with those of his comrades, kept pilots and machines in serviceable order in the most adverse conditions.

George Samuel Hynes was born in 1895, in Liverpool. There, he served an apprenticeship as a marine engineer and joined the Royal Flying Corps at the beginning of the First World War. Three of his brothers also served in the army, on the Western Front. His career with the RFC began at Farnborough and after several postings he travelled out to Egypt with No. 14 Squadron. Within a year or two he was living in the deserts of Arabia in either canvas hangars or bell tents in advanced landing grounds from which X Flight aircraft flew on reconnaissance, bombing and strafing missions.

Few histories of the early wars in the desert recount the contributions made by men other than the commissioned officers. Often their individuality and their contributions are lumped together in expressions such as the following as it was applied to No. 14 Squadron, to which X belonged. 'As well as the necessary Air Mechanics and Fitters, the party included Royal Army Medical Corps and Army Service Corps personnel.' In fact, to be fair, the officers, the fliers, have seldom been mentioned either because there is so little in the public domain about X Flight itself.

On the other hand, in his famous books, Lawrence occasionally mentions other ranks by name. For example in *Revolt in the Desert*, he did pay particular tribute to his sergeants, Stokes and Lewis, for whom he had particular admiration. Nevertheless, Lawrence confessed in the *Seven Pillars of Wisdom* that their real names were not Stokes and Lewis – 'Their names may have been Yells and Brooke, but became Lewis and Stokes after their jealously-loved tools' (the Stokes 3-inch portable mortar and the famous Lewis machine gun). George too writes about other ranks as well as the officers, the pilots whom he admired and whose aircraft he scrupulously serviced to keep safe.

In his memoirs, George writes about Lawrence over and over again, mostly in a spirited defence of the great man's reputation; but here, in this account, I have mentioned the great man only in relation to X Flight. I have selected only those pages relating to George's actual personal experiences with X Flight in order to present a narrative account of the deeds of that covert group of men and machines.

Although as a boy I visited Uncle George, along with my father, his brother, listening to both men's war stories and looking at his notes and his drawings, it was not until 2008 that I heard of his memoirs. Years later, in the late 1950s, he had laboriously typed some 220 pages of them. For the privilege of reading through them I thank my cousin, his daughter, Mrs Ellen Gannicott who gave me copies. Although I knew of the letters which T.E.L. had written to George, we had no idea where they had ended up until I discovered that they are now held by the Houghton Library of Harvard University along with a sixteen-page 'synopsis' written by my uncle. Ellen had retained photocopies and typescript copies of those letters but none of the surviving family had known that the originals had been sold at Sotheby's in 1961 to an American buyer.

Although George had met with, spoken with and sometimes worked with Lawrence, he was no closer to that enigmatic man than any other person had ever been. He wrote much in defence of Lawrence but others have done that and George would not have known anything about the 'behind-the-scenes' politics. On the other hand, George's recollections of his service in the air force have the immediacy of personal involvement. They are written in unpretentious language, the language of one who left a senior elementary school at age fourteen and went on to take City and Guilds qualifications in marine engineering. I have edited his writings but in so doing, out of respect for him, I have tried to retain his style. Therefore in editing and presenting George's script I have tried to keep as closely as possible to his vernacular and personal narrative style.

Whilst he, the son of a man who had himself served as a regular soldier, was serving in the Middle East, his three brothers were serving on the Western Front and George was well aware that they were having a worse time than he was. His eldest brother John served with the Liverpool Irish right through major battles from 1914 to 1919 and in his post-war years suffered from the effects of gas poisoning. A slightly younger brother, James, served first with the Connaught Rangers until after they had sustained extraordinarily high casualties, when he was transferred to the Inniskillings, dying of wounds in Germany in the last week of the war. Their younger brother Richard, my father, served in the trenches for two years with the Lancashire Fusiliers, sustaining a trench knife scar.

There is such a wide variety of different renditions of place names in books and documents relating to the war in the Middle East that, in the interests of consistency, I have favoured the spellings used by X Flight's commanding officers in their weekly reports. For example, George uses the place name Desi whereas it is written, DECIE, in capitals, as were all place names in X Flight reports. George's Guweira gives way to GUEIRA. In fact, back in 1926 arguments about the spelling of Arabic place names took place between Lawrence and his publisher's proofreaders, one of whom complained that the manuscript of *Revolt in the Desert* was 'full of inconsistencies in the spelling of proper names, a point which reviewers often take up'.

Lawrence replied with, 'Arabic names won't go into English exactly, for their consonants are not the same as ours, and their vowels, like ours, vary from district to district.' He then goes on to tease the editor unmercifully as he picks up on other spelling inconsistencies.

I have unravelled George's stories in an attempt to set them in chronological order. He wrote his memoirs more or less in a time sequence but not strictly so because most often he wrote down his memories as they spontaneously occurred to him.

In presenting this book I quote George directly:

> I have endeavoured to give my personal experience in my writing this book alone without any contacts with any person who had served in the Middle East campaign during the 1914 War or any person who served under Lawrence during the Arab Revolt, 1916/18.

In the event that his memoirs might be published, George wished to dedicate it to the memory of a surgeon, Dr Fosebrooke, of Broadgreen Hospital, Liverpool, a former prisoner of war of the Japanese. George expressed his gratitude for an operation he underwent in 1952. He also wished to remember all who joined in a defence of Lawrence's reputation.

Little has been written about the contribution made by X Flight whose aircraft and personnel in its close support operations worked for several years in adverse conditions in advanced desert landing grounds. In particular, the existence and deeds of X Flight were kept so secret that in fact, for most of the time, the Royal Air Force Paymaster received no pay returns and consequently the airmen who served with the flight received neither back pay nor hardship allowances because no records of their entitlements were kept!

George wrote:

> I have often been asked why no Royal Flying Corps personnel were recorded in the *Seven Pillars of Wisdom*, and why British aircraft were not shown in the recent film, as the inquirers were rather put out about it.

He went on to say that X Flight was not added to the list of the British units because as soon as the Turks had surrendered the Flight had been immediately ordered out taking all equipment, aircraft and personnel to Egypt. Flight members were given some pay and ten days' leave in Cairo, returning to their new base on Armistice Day 1918. On that day, the officers joined the NCOs in the Sergeants' Mess for a celebration until two in the morning when all ended up in the Officers' Mess.

George surmised that Lawrence too was unable to obtain a list of X Flight's personnel. Perhaps he was right, because if the Paymaster in England never admitted owing back pay then even he himself had no list either. George said that he kept his own list but so far it has not turned up in his documents.

Of that 'special' Flight, Bragger and Wright's publication *Lawrence's Air Force* had only this to say, 'In September 1917, 14 Squadron sent X Flight under the command of Captain Stent to Akaba, to continue the fight against the Turks, but that is another story.'[1]

This, in fact, is that other story.

James P. Hynes
June 2010

NOTES

1 Bragger, R. & Wright, P., 'Lawrence's Air Force', in the *Cross and Cockade*, summer 2003.

Introduction

Much has been written by and about Lawrence of Arabia but little has ever been written about the handful of aircraft and personnel of X Flight, which was set up to give him and his Arab army close air support.

Lawrence and the Arabs wrecked many trains, stations and railway lines but so too did X Flight with their bombs and machine-guns in regular daily support of the irregulars. Consequently, Lawrence held the Royal Flying Corps/the Royal Air Force in high regard. He wrote, with conviction and accuracy, 'It was the R.A.F., which had converted the Turkish retreat into rout, which had abolished their telephone and telegraph connections, had blocked their lorry columns, scattered their infantry units.'[1]

The capture of the town of Akaba by Lawrence and the Arabs on 6 July 1917 enabled X Flight to set up its principal base there, from which flying operations were conducted and a succession of small advance landing grounds could be supplied with aircraft and skilled personnel. Akaba was the last port the Turks held on the Red Sea and its loss led the way to their ultimate defeat as did the £200,000 a month Lawrence was spending to encourage the Arabs to revolt against the Turks. Lawrence's personality was charismatic but so too was the gold which Britain allowed him to distribute!

Early in the conflict Lawrence asked for air support and he got it from both No. 1 Squadron of the Australian Air Force and the Royal Flying Corps. Dedicated help was always available to him throughout the campaign from 14 Squadron of the Royal Flying Corps between 3 February 1915 and 4 February 1919 with its HQ first in Ismailia then Deir el Belah, mid-1916, and thence Junction Station in 1917. Close support was provided by a detachment of C Flight in the Hejaz from December 1916 to August 1917, in its raid on the Hejaz railway at Ma'an from Sinai in August 1917. But the closest support of all, for him and his Arab allies, was provided by the secret X Flight with its aircraft, the Tiyaras, the 'female flying things' which so impressed the Bedouin.

Formed at Shoreham on 3 February 1915, No. 14 Squadron, commanded by Major G. B. Stopford, had sailed out from England to Egypt on the liner, SS *Anchises* on 7 November 1915. Although some sources give SS *Anchises* as the transport vessel, an intriguing note by George Hynes gives an SS *Hunsgrove* (commandeered from the Germans and previously called the SS *Lorenzo*) as the

1

ship which set out with 14 Squadron and full equipment for 'an unknown destination' (the Dardanelles) but was diverted from Malta to Egypt instead. He claimed that during the voyage the crew successfully fought off a U-boat attack using Lewis guns and four rifles! There were a number of former German vessels commandeered in Suez at the beginning of the war and all were renamed, all having the prefix 'Hun' (some naval or Whitehall jest possibly) when put into service as British vessels. Among such vessels were SS *Huntsvale* (formerly *Barenfels*); *Huntsend* (formerly *Lutzow*); *Hunsbrook* (*Annaberg*); *Huntsfall* (*Goslar*); *Huntsmoor* (*Rostock*); and HMT *Huntsgreen* (*Derflinger*).

Flights were established in Kantara and Ismailia before Christmas and by then a detachment was also operating in the western desert of Egypt participating in the Battle of Mersa Matruh on Christmas Day 1915.

Just after Christmas they moved out of Heliopolis to Ismailia near the Suez Canal and months later became part of the Middle East Brigade formed on 1 April 1916 by which time Salmond was a Brigadier General. Exactly two years later to the day, the RFC became the RAF. At the time the squadron was equipped with BE2c machines and a few Martinsydes. The BE2cs played the biggest role supporting Lawrence.The RFC's duties lay in Army co-operation in Egypt, Arabia and Palestine. In his memoirs George Hynes commented:

> I do know that Geoffrey Salmond had a hard time building up the Middle East from our first Squadron, No. 14, and our brotherly squadron, No. 1 Australian on the front line....

During the early years of the war in the Middle East, General Sir Archibald Murray had led the Egyptian Expeditionary Force (EEF). His forces had pushed across the Sinai constructing railway and freshwater lines from the Suez Canal to support operations on the southern edge of Palestine, south of Gaza. Under his direction, two attempts were made to capture Gaza: the First Battle of Gaza on 26 March and the Second Battle of Gaza on 19 April. Both attempts were embarrassing failures so the War Office replaced Murray on 28 June 1917 with General Allenby who saw the war in the Middle East through to the end.

Air support for Allenby's ground forces was placed in the care of Brigadier General A. E. Borton, in December 1917, when he took command of the Palestine Brigade comprising two wings: the 5th Wing and the 40th Army Wing. The Counter-Air and interdiction roles were carried out by 40 Wing, while 5th Wing squadrons were mainly involved with tactical reconnaissance and artillery direction whilst also taking part in bombing raids against Ottoman positions. By mid-summer 1918, the Brigade also had a balloon company, an engine repair depot and an aircraft park and depot. One solitary Handley Page O/400 was added to the strength.

The Germans and the Turks with their Rumpler and Fokker aircraft, superior in design and performance, had exercised air superiority in the Levant so Allenby set out to challenge that by increasing the number and quality of the British machines.

It was a slow process and the RFC gained the upper hand by the sheer dedication and determination of the pilots and ground staff working with aircraft which needed a lot of 'make do and mend'.

The enemy comprised the Turkish Fourth Army, commanded by the German General Friedrich Freiherr Kress von Kressenstein defending Palestine, while in Mesopotamia the main Turkish force was commanded by another German, General Erich von Falkenhayn, who was attempting to recapture Baghdad from the British. Although Turkish troops had won several victories against the British, their morale was poor because of severe shortages of food for both animals and men, ammunition and transport. Many deserted and eventually they lost to the British and Empire armies together with Feisal and his Arabs.

The tactically brilliant capture of Akaba by Lawrence and the Arabs on 6 July 1917 was a significant day for X Flight because for the rest of the war the RFC landing ground there was the Flight's centre of operations. A number of covert advanced landing grounds were set up out of Akaba and George Hynes spent much of his war in them.

In the Third Battle of Gaza, fought between 31 October and 7 November 1917 in southern Palestine, British Empire forces under Allenby broke the Turkish Gaza–Beersheba line. Australian Light Horse captured the town of Beersheba on the first day and from then on the war went badly for the Turks.

During the conflict, army commanders and air commanders learned how to work together fighting desert battles in which flying machines played an increasingly important role, not only in photographic reconnaissance in communication but also in action as weapons of war. Conditions under which men and machines worked in those deserts were very trying indeed. The hazards faced by airmen of the RFC back in England were bad enough but No. 14 Squadron had to face them in the unforgiving deserts of Egypt and Arabia.

For example, No. 14 Squadron and X Flight itself carried out some night flying where advance landing grounds were no more than hardened mud or sand, strewn with small rocks set between hazardous hills. That was a remarkable achievement when one considers the criticisms made about night flying conditions in England itself where, 'The chief complaints against aerodromes and night landing places were that they were insufficient in number, some of them too small, and some of them unsafe by reason of the surface being rough, such as ridge and furrow, or intersected by hedgerows or dykes.'[2]

Furthermore, in England, 'Night-flying is, as far as possible, forbidden at aerodromes where the state of the surface is such as to present unusual difficulties on landing system is inferior to the French and German systems.'[3]

So much for the hazards of night flying in Britain but even worse the document pointed out that at the beginning of the Great War 'the question of using aeroplanes for more than reconnaissance and observing artillery fire, as also the important part machine guns were going to play both in the air and on land, had hardly been considered.'

3

'The provision of machine guns for cavalry regiments and infantry battalions was also seriously inadequate because no thought had been given to providing them for aeroplanes.' Given the absence of machine guns pilots and observers took to using rifles in their aircraft. Things very gradually began to improve:

> The provision of weapons such as machine guns, bombs, hand grenades, darts, &c, fell under the able hand of the Master-General of the Ordnance; and the Committee are unable to find any delay on the part of the Royal Flying Corps in making use of any of these, or in providing mountings, racks, &c, for them, within a reasonable time of their being allotted to the Corps.[4]

The document went on to say that experiments had to be made to find the most suitable way of carrying the several war requirements in aeroplanes. The pilots and ground crews of X Flight of necessity carried out many such experiments in the harsh environments of the desert. Fortunately they suffered no casualties as a result.

Another recommendation that pilots should be provided with proper maps, compasses or altimeters was impossible in Arabia as there were none. They did not exist. X Flight had to make their own maps and the maps for the ground forces. In fact their principal duty was flying daily reconnaissance taking thousands of photographs of enemy-held territory. The German and Turkish aircraft in their turn were doing exactly the same thing. During the course of the war British and German aircrews took tens of thousands of photographs between them.

The huge contrasts between high day and low night temperatures in Arabia made aeroplane maintenance a constant problem as woodwork shrank and warped. Machines had to be constantly stripped down and serviced. Spares and replacement parts, never plentiful, were often found to be useless. Fortunately X Flight's machines, fitted with 90-hp Royal Aircraft Factory air-cooled engines, gave comparatively little trouble but the water-cooled Hispano-Suiza and Beardmores boiled water away. Oils sometimes became so hot they were rendered useless.

Although the RFC's principal duties lay in just that, flying, there in the deserts, they had to make regular and constant use of motorised transport together with camels, horses and mules. The ubiquitous Crossley tenders fitted with double wheels were used so often that the RFC might aptly have been called the Royal Flying and Motoring Corps!

Air Mechanic George spent his war repairing and maintaining some second rate aircraft which X Flight had to put up with during its secret operations in the desert wastes. Of course he was devoted to engineering and took pride in his skills with those early flying machines but he was also fascinated by the horses and camels which were used so skilfully by the Arabs who lived in those deserts.

The expression, 'knights of the air' as applied to combat pilots has become a journalistic cliché but it was an apt metaphor for the fliers in the deserts of Arabia. Medieval knights, almost exclusively the sons of nobility, were trained to make gallant use of their weapons on the field of combat. Strict codes of conduct and chivalry were expected of them and captive knights were to be treated well, ransomed and not insulted or killed. Similar rules were followed in the deserts of Arabia. Captive officer pilots were treated well by captor officers who were ready to 'buy' prisoners from the Bedouin whose rules of chivalry were not the same! Fliers wisely carried gold pieces with them to pay the Arabs to hand them over into care.

If then the pilots were the knights, the mechanics were the squires. The mechanics kept the knights' weapons in good order, handing them over to the knights as they went into battle and repairing them when damaged in combat. Like the knights of old, the pilots were from the top of the social hierarchy, the products of expensive schools and formal education whereas the mechanics, the squires, were from the artisan classes, the craftsmen.

Almost exclusively the aircraft were referred to as 'machines', both in formal reports and in conversations. In formal reports the pilots were described as being 'on' a machine, not 'in' a machine. For example an extract from a formal X Flight document reported, 'Divers on a B.E. 2E flew Col. Lawrence to EL JAFAR for the latter to attend an important conference, returning after 2 hours.'

Perhaps within that usage there lay a residual memory of being 'on' a horse, because one does not ride 'in' a horse. Of course many early RFC pilots had first been cavalry officers!

Occasionally the mechanics like squires became knights themselves but even when they became 'very perfect gentle knights' like Chaucer's hero they were sometimes ostracised because they had risen from the wrong social class. The remarkable air ace James McCudden VC, with fifty-seven victories, who started his RFC career as a mechanic was reportedly turned down for command of No. 85 Squadron RAF because of his lack of a public school education!

George showed the greatest respect for the pilots and indeed for all his comrades, and he like so many others, admired Lawrence for his lack of 'side' for his ease in the company of rankers and his readiness to pull down the mighty from their thrones. Many pages in George's memoirs were written in defence of Lawrence's reputation. He was particularly angered by the criticisms made by Richard Adlington in his book *Lawrence of Arabia: A Biographical Enquiry* published in 1955. Others with more scholarship resources available to them have argued their cases for and against the great Lawrence. That is not the purpose of this book. This is actually the story of X Flight as experienced by an airman who served with that secret unit in support of Lawrence and the Arab Revolt.

During the 1930s, George corresponded with the 'new' Lawrence, Aircraftsman Shaw of the Royal Air Force. Two letters from Shaw to George Hynes are now held in the Houghton Library at Harvard and in one of those letters there appears a telling sentence which may not have been confessed elsewhere, 'Parts of our war were not so bad, I suppose, though personally I hated it.'

NOTES

1 Lawrence, T. E., *Seven Pillars of Wisdom*, Chapter CXIII.

2 *Flight*, 4 January 1917, given under the subheading: 'CHARGE 7.—VARIOUS DEFECTS IN AERODROMES AND SYSTEM OF LIGHTING LANDING GROUNDS', paragraphs 97, 103 and 106.

3 Ibid.

4 Ibid.

Lawrence of Arabia's Secret Air Force

GEORGE JOINS THE ROYAL FLYING CORPS

In 1914 George Samuel Hynes was serving as a third engineer on a floating workshop run by H & C Grayson Ltd, Shipbuilders and Engineers of Liverpool. He left, made several attempts to join the Mounted Engineers and the Navy as an artificer but eventually enrolled in the Royal Flying Corps formed just two years earlier in 1912. The RFC became the British military air arm whose chief duties were supporting the Army, spotting for artillery and flying on photographic reconnaissance.

In an article in the *Liverpool Echo and Evening Post* printed on 28 February 1963, George recalled his recruitment:

> I joined the old Royal Flying Corps in 1914 as a boy of 19 and became an apprentice engineer. They sent me to Egypt in 1915 with No. 14 Squadron, who were flying biplanes carrying bombs and machine guns.

Formed at Shoreham on 3 February 1915, No. 14 Squadron, commanded by Lt Col Geoffrey Salmond, had sailed out from England to Egypt on the liner, SS *Anchises* on 7 November 1915. Just after Christmas they moved out of Heliopolis to Ismailia near the Suez Canal, becoming part of the Middle East Brigade formed on 1 April 1916, by which time Salmond was a Brigadier General. At the time the Squadron was equipped with Farman biplanes and a few Martinsydes.

His early RFC service was spent in Farnborough, Hounslow, Shoreham and Gosport before his posting overseas. In his memoirs he mentions being on sentry duty at Hounslow aerodrome in May 1915 when he had to deal with an intruder. He probably went out to Egypt with the Squadron in November 1915 as he mentions a near miss attack by a submarine.

From the outset the RFC expected high standards of fitness, skill, character and behaviour in its recruits and personnel. George wrote:

> Discipline was so strong that my Squadron when stationed at Hounslow No. 14 was presented with white woollen gloves as a mark of respect by a titled lady, for the noticeable behaviour in their association with the opposite sex

during their term of duties in that area. Permission was given to wear them in public in place of the Army issue in khaki wool.

Whilst in the Middle East, he served with the Squadron in Heliopolis, Ismailia, Arabia, back in Ismailia, the advance on Sinai Peninsula, then Gaza and finally the Special Duty X Flight in Arabia until 28 October 1918.

In either December 1915 or January 1916, George was in Cairo when a revolt broke out among students and members of the Egyptian Army. A few RFC Crossley tenders were sent into the city manned by comrades armed with machine guns and rifles to patrol the streets. Of course the Flying Corps used machines designed for use in the air, then in the Middle East, they soon found that in order to do that efficiently they had to make regular and frequent use of Crossley tenders, camels and horses on land! In 1913, the 20 hp Crossley tenders were put into service with the new RFC and by 1918 they had over 6,000 of them adapted for use as staff cars, tenders and ambulances.

A former commanding officer of X Flight, V.D. Siddons, thought very highly of those Crossleys. In his summary of X Flight operations for the week ending 12 January 1918, Akaba, he wrote, 'For rough country, the Crossley Light Tender with double wheels all round is an ideal car and is superior to any other type down here, namely: Rolls-Royce, Talbot, new type pattern and Ford.'

In Cairo, George was amused by the fact that the wives of the Sultan of Egypt often passed through the streets in a fleet of red motor cars with red motorcycle escorts on their way to the fun fair, Lunar Park, on Thursdays when the grounds were closed to the public!

AN EARLY NO. 14 SQUADRON INCIDENT

From the outset, No. 14 Squadron engaged in fairly routine tasks such as photographic reconnaissance and occasional sorties to pick up downed pilots or to bomb and strafe the enemy in support of ground troops. One such desert rescue is recounted in a copy of the magazine *Flight*:

> In May 1916, machines from No. 14 rescued Lieutenant (Later Sir Pierre) Van Ryneveld, who had been forced landed in the Sinai desert. [Van Ryneveld was serving in the South African Aviation Corps. In 1920 he became Director of Air Services in South Africa.][1]

The article continues:

> About the same time Lt. Kingsley forced-landed on a flat mountaintop in South Sinai. The pilot repaired the engine while his observer kept the Turks at bay with a rear gun. Eventually the pilot took off, diving over the mountain side after a too short run and flew back home.

George mentions an amusing incident when he was in Ismailia on or about 5 June 1916:

One morning an Egyptian newsboy came to the camp to sell the *Egyptian Mail*. The boy was shouting as he sold his papers, 'Berry good news dis mornin. Kitchener dead, berry good news!'

George continues:

> It was a great surprise to us that Lord Kitchener had met his death on the destroyer that was taking him to Russia, and a shock; but the boys were amused to hear the newsboy declare it as 'berry good news'.

George concluded that some Tommy must have played a trick on the newsboy coaching him to shout that it was very good news!

The Squadron's early brush with the enemy took place on 18 June 1916, when its aircraft bombed and strafed German Rumpler C1 bomber/rec, two-seaters and Pfalz EII single-seat escort aircraft at El Arish in the Sinai. Eleven British aircraft, eight from No. 14 Squadron and the rest from No. 17, successfully bombed the site. Three aircraft failed to return; one pilot was captured but later managed to escape; a second managed to take to the air again after a forced landing and the third landed in the sea but was rescued.[2]

GEORGE IN ISMAILIA

George's comments about General Murray may have reflected the views of all the common soldiers out in the Middle East when he wrote:

> I had a good look at Murray when he arrived at Ismailiya [Ismailia] to award the Military Cross to Lt Yates only a couple of weeks after Yates had struck a heavy blow against the Turks with his two, one hundred pound bombs. Murray surrounded by professional military and intelligence experts depended a lot on the photographs taken by our aircraft.
>
> Murray liked the Indian type of pomp and ceremony so when he arrived he was escorted by the Bengal Lancers. He stood in front of us and when he walked along our ranks during 'close inspection', he passed through with hardly a look at our unit on parade.
>
> We also knew that within twenty-four hours General Murray was being sent home and shortly afterwards, Allenby was on his way out in a British destroyer. A rumour broke out that our troops had taken Gaza but someone had given the order to retire but nobody knew who.
>
> I was fortunate enough to be on duty, alone, in a tent on guard and acting as telephone orderly. A field telephone had been rigged to convey messages directly to Cairo. An officer pilot and his observer reported that there were signs of evacuation of Turkish troops from El Arish.

A TRIBUTE TO ALLENBY

George comments:

> Allenby reacted very quickly saying he would not attack Gaza until he had plenty of guns. Soon they were rolling out to him. Although the press called

him 'The Bull' he was a gentleman in looking after the welfare of his men making sure he had enough weapons to finish the job. Allenby put the full weight of his mounted troops into battle along with Salmond, with every available aircraft raining hell on the retreating enemy. His greatest friend in that enterprise was the amateur soldier, Thomas Edward Lawrence, without doubt or contradiction.

Allenby speedily livened up the Cairo Savoy headquarters, joining his new army in the field and making sure he got more staff into the field with the army where they belonged. It had come to our ears that there were far too many staff officers winning military crosses for their services in Cairo!

Allenby, showed that he was a soldier who was active in the field, not back in an office. He went on to demand guns, guns and more guns for his army and they began rolling off the railway tracks at night strengthening the only two Pom Pom guns that had no doubt been relics of the Boer War.

Across 3/4 August 1916, the Squadron helped Anzac troops repulse Turkish troops in battle near Romani by directing artillery fire, bombing and strafing and harassing them back to El Arish. On 5 August an unnamed crew shot down an enemy Rumpler but 2/Lieuts Hursthouse and McDiarmid in a BE.2c (Bleriot Experimental) were wounded. On 10 August, another BE was brought down by both ground fire and an attack by two Rumplers. 2/Lieut Edwards received several wounds. His observer, who was about to go on leave, had been shot through the chest but when an ambulance arrived he refused treatment until he had given his report but the unfortunate airman then died.[3]

Although the Arabs would not allow Christian troops into the region, in October 1916, C Flight along with six machines and appropriate personnel were allowed to set up in Rabegh on the eastern coast Red Sea after leaving El Qantara. By December 1916 the Turks had abandoned El Arish where they had previously deployed 160 Rumplers, mechanically superior to the aircraft used by the British.

LAWRENCE AND AIRCRAFT SUPPORT NEAR WEJH

Lawrence could paint a vivid picture of some of the Squadron's activities using a broader brush than George whose knowledge was immediate and rather more restricted within his own personal experiences. For example, Lawrence expresses his admiration of the pilots in the following accounts of air action carried out by No. 14 Squadron back in 1916:

We could also prick the Turks into discomfort by asking General Salmond for his promised long-distance air raid on Maan. As it was difficult, Salmond had chosen Stent, with other tried pilots of Rabegh or Wejh, and told them to do their best. They had experience of forced landing on desert surfaces and could pick out an unknown destination across unmapped hills: Stent spoke

Arabic perfectly. The flight had to be air-contained, but its commander was full of resource and display, like other bundles of nerves, who, to punish themselves, did outrageous things. On this occasion he ordered low flying, to make sure the aim; and profited by reaching Maan, and dropping thirty-two bombs in and about the unprepared station. Two bombs into the barracks killed thirty-five men and wounded fifty. Eight struck the engine-shed, heavily damaging the plant and stock. A bomb in the General's kitchen finished his cook and his breakfast. Four fell on the aerodrome. Despite the shrapnel our pilots and engines returned safely to their temporary landing ground at Kuntilla above Akaba. That afternoon they patched the machines, and after dark slept under their wings. In the following dawn they were off once more, three of them this time, to Aba el Lissan, where the sight of the great camp had made Stent's mouth water. They bombed the horse lines and stampeded the animals, visited the tents and scattered the Turks. As on the day before, they flew low and were much hit, but not fatally. Long before noon they were back in Kuntilla.[4]

JANUARY 1917

George describes an incident when two of the Squadron's aircraft were shot down by ground fire in the first month of 1917, although he mistakenly wrote Seagraves instead of Seward.

> We had two Martinsydes shot down, Captain Kingsley and Lieutenant Seagraves. They had gone low over their target and heavy rifle fire did the damage.
> During that attack our chief in command Geoffrey Salmond flew his own machine a B.E. 2c over with them to direct the operation as he was not the type to sit at the Savoy Hotel like General Murray and his staff. He was as keen as the pilots in the front to see that the work went as planned. He played a very important part in capturing El Arish and Rafa and resulted in a General Allenby coming to join us later.

George writes:

> Captain Kingsley I think was rescued but Lieutenant Seagraves burnt his machine, jumped into the Med and swam back to our lines. I did hear that some Arabs and Australians came to Kingsley's rescue and must mention that Kingsley was one of the rankers of the early pilots of the Royal Flying Corps at the outbreak of the War with such as Sergeant Dismore, McCrane and McCudden, Lieutenant Lorraine (Bobby Lorraine, the actor) the first pilot injured in France and later our pilot instructor.

This latter, Lt Col Robert Lorraine, RAF, DSO, MC, was an exceedingly controversial person, a man about whom *Flight* magazine's obituary in January 1936 said:

For his first aircraft he decided to purchase a Blériot machine and went to France in April 1910 to learn to fly at Blériot's base at Pau. It was in his diary at this time that he used the term 'joystick' in describing the aircraft's control column – the first recorded use of the term.

Lorraine was born on 14 January 1876 in New Brighton, Merseyside, England, and died on 23 December 1935 in London.

An account of the same incident in *Flight* magazine gives more detail about Seward:

> In the beginning of 1917 after the evacuation of El Arish and when the pipeline was being laid across the desert, Lt Seward was hit by 'Archies' near Gaza. He descended into the sea to prevent his machine being captured. On being fired at by the Turks, he swam further out to sea, then for four hours followed the coast, and eventually landed exhausted, being picked up by one of our own cavalry patrols.[5]

George comments:

> Rather surprisingly, those two officers were posted a couple of days later. Then six weeks later, Captain Dempsey who was reported as having been shot down arrived in reporting that he had landed at El Arish, toured it and found Captain Tipton's engine in the Turkish drome. Captain Tipton had been shot down by rifle fire during our first big raid on El Arish aerodrome when seven of the enemy and hangars had been destroyed.

The Germans were forced to leave Beersheba in February 1917.

When with No. 14 Squadron in Kilo 143, Egypt, George got talking with a Jew, aged about thirty, who was in charge of labourers working for the RFC. The Jewish man told George that his family, wife and children were being cared for in a Catholic convent back in Palestine, looked after by the Sisters. He went on to say that he had volunteered for the job otherwise he would have been conscripted into the Turkish Army. The very effective Australian No. 1 Squadron formed in January 1916 was also stationed in Kilo 143 between January 1917 and March 1917 and like X Flight had to manage with machines which were much inferior to those flying for the Germans! Furthermore like 14 Squadron and its fledgling X Flight, its principal task was that of long range photo-reconnaissance, which involved deep penetrations into enemy territory.[6] Two years previously, in 1915, Colonel Borton, of the RFC remarked, 'Our daily reconnaissance is a positive torture,' and so it remained throughout the conflict.[7]

X FLIGHT AND THE FIRST BATTLE OF GAZA

According to George, two X Flight pilots saved the British infantry from defeat in battle. However, the evidence seems to be that although those pilots did drive off some Turkish cavalry in pursuit of retreating troops the First Battle of Gaza had already turned into an ignominious defeat. Although George gives no date for his story the details point towards that first Battle of Gaza on Monday 26 March 1917.

In all during the campaign, three attacks were made on Gaza by British and Commonwealth troops but the first two failed badly. The third and last attack on Gaza in November 1917 successfully followed the capture of Beersheba on the first day by the Australian Light Horse.

George wrote:

> The attack on Gaza was kept very quiet and we in the ranks of the Royal Flying Corps, at the foremost operational ground at Rafa, never told what was being planned. Fortunately under Salmond, our pilots did know but they kept to a very high standard of confidentiality to avoid the enemy obtaining any information.
>
> It was not until about seven thirty that morning of the setback to our army that we got the whole story. Our troops had attacked Gaza and during the night under cover of darkness in 'stocking feet', had taken it. From dawn with the first rays of the sun, our aircraft gave every support to the army. Suddenly it all changed when I was on the ground with my mates receiving, refuelling and bombing up for rapid continuous support to the advancing troops. The first machine to arrive back was that of Captain Freeman, our flight commander.

This latter must have been Wilfrid, later Air Vice Marshal Sir Wilfrid Rhodes Freeman FGCB, DSO & MC (Baronet in 1945), who was with No. 14 Squadron at one time. He played a big role in the rearmament of the RAF in the inter-war years.

The citation for his award of the Military Cross reads:

> Lieutenant W. R. Freeman, The Manchester Regiment and Royal Flying Corps. For gallantry, ability, and very valuable work performed. Located the position of German batteries on 10th instant, and conveyed the information by wireless messages from his aeroplane to our Artillery, and, although his propeller and planes were pierced by the enemy's bullets, he remained aloft for more than five hours during the day.[8]

George continues:

> I now remember how two of our pilots saved a total collapse of that attack. Captain Freeman, the first one arriving at the drome, would not accept a drink of tea as he paced up and down. He jumped out of his machine and called out, 'I don't know what it has gone wrong because our troops are retreating like rabbits. Get ready to strip the hangars in case of a quick move to the rear.
>
> Just as he completed that statement, another aircraft landed, taxied up to us and out jumped Captain Wilberforce [possibly Captain W.R.S.

Wilberforce, King's Royal Rifle Corps attached to the RAF], the pilot and commander of B Flight. He said, 'The Turkish cavalry are cutting across the plain from Beersheba to complete a massacre. Bomb up our machines at once.'

Captain Freeman then shouted, 'Load us up with 20 pounders at once and quickly!' and we set to as our bombs were ready detonated in our hangars and both Freeman and Wilberforce set off in less than three minutes on a straight course, not for those Gaza hills but bearing off across a small sand dune covered with green scrub like palm. They headed straight for Beersheeba to stop that cavalry charge between us and the retiring remnants of our army.

They raced across our drome at Raffa [Rafa], took off with fresh bomb loads from in the direction of Beersheba, returning about twenty minutes later saying, 'All's well we have smashed them up and rest assured we have helped our boys to escape!' The drome then settled down as if it never happened.

The two pilots got back later after totally breaking up the Turkish cavalry and satisfied that their machines had given them a grip on the situation. It must be recorded that those two pilots had saved not only a big panic in Whitehall but a big reversal in the war in the Sinai campaign.

The pilots were very upset, as were all of the pilots and staff at Cairo, at the sufferings borne by the Manchesters. It hit Freeman particularly hard as it involved the boys from his own Manchester territorial units who had been badly cut up in that calamity.

During that first assault on Gaza all units, including artillery, advanced during the night crossing the deep Wadi Ghuzze. The advance, which began at 2.30 on the morning of Monday the 26th, was hindered by a thick fog which did not lift until 8 a.m. The mounted troops did very well indeed but infantry fared very badly. The 1st Battalion, of the Manchester (Machine-Gun) Regiment did take part and in fact George's brother, Richard, began his service with them but was transferred to the Lancashire Fusiliers for action on the Western Front.

The 53rd Division had to attack across exposed ground through shrapnel, machine gun and rifle fire. Although they gained advantage towards the end of the day, the British Command, Dobell and Chetwode, called off the attack and that retreat witnessed by the pilots began. That decision to retire dismayed most of their soldiers.

George continues:

I often wondered how those two got on later as they saved the day by going into the attack with their bombs, smashing the Turkish cavalry. They saved a total retreat by our troops. In fact we heard that the whole Field Ambulance Unit was taken prisoner and many thousands of badly wounded men went through our base field hospital.

In recalling the setting up of one of the advance landing grounds in support of attacking Australian troops, probably an attack on Gaza, George wrote:

> My pilot, my CO, gave me his instructions for the day while I was able to look around and met my squadron pal, Air Mechanic Pendrons, another engine mechanic who had been selected to move up with the advancing Aussies where he was in charge of a camel caravan with petrol, bombs and other necessities for laying out our landing strip.
>
> The rear party of the patrols cleared casualties from the ground in order to give us clear uncluttered ground for our aircraft to land and take off. Pendrons and I began by filling up our machines and arranging the landing of another advance party machine returning for refuelling and bombing up. All day machines from our rear base passed over with their loads of destruction giving every support to our combined infantry and cavalry, light horsemen expert in desert warfare.

Major Bannatyne, an early Commanding Officer of No. 14 Squadron, RFC, had left Egypt for Arabia to explore possible landing grounds at Rabegh. HMS *Dufferin*, then anchored in the Red Sea, was used as his HQ. No. 14 Squadron arrived in Rabegh in November 1916, probably on the 17th. No troops were landed because, said a message from Cairo, there were too many Christians in the expeditionary force! (Turkish forces continued to press slowly forward by attempting to 'buy in' Arab tribes.)

However, the RFC was allowed in on 12 November. C Flight of No. 14 Squadron embarked at Suez for Arabia in support of the Hejaz Expeditionary Force. The Flight Commander was Major A.J. Ross DSO, who was fluent in Arabic. No. 14 Squadron's motto, an extract from the Qur'an, was written in Arabic. It translates as, 'I spread my wings and keep my promise.'

George continues:

> Pendrons and I decided to make some tea as he had brought some rations of tea with him along with a tin of milk, sugar and a bottle of water sufficient for his journey.
>
> Having made a small fire from scrub brush we boiled our bottle of water in his billy can, enough for a pint of tea, but after making the tea, we got a terrible surprise as we poured in the milk. We gazed at our brew as we witnessed the milk had changed to purple! It then dawned on us that the disinfectant tablets in the bottle of water had changed the usual milky colour to purple but we went on anyway and enjoyed our cuppa.
>
> We were surprised to see one lone enemy machine fly over our ground while we were eating and circle at about eight thousand feet. We sat and continued our meal waiting for his bombs to drop but none was dropped so we expected later to have an attack but none came to interfere with our own operations. The enemy left in the direction of Beersheba.

From about three o'clock in the afternoon, we were busy keeping our machines on the go with increased support in the air from our rear base as about eight Martinsydes flew over loaded with one hundred pounders and twenty pounders. We heard the crash of bombs dropped from low altitudes that helped to defeat the enemy before our Aussies went in for the final attack.

A little later we jumped into our kite and took off in the trail of the other machines at about 1,000 feet. It was cool but there was no wind but it was bumpy ride as we landed at our base and without any gear which I had left on the landing ground the night before. My greatcoat and water bottle were returned to me later by an Australian patrol. That was my first flight over the enemy lines and because of it I can claim to be the first ranker to be air gunner in operations in the Sinai.

APRIL 1917

On 22 April 1917, Major Ross handed over command of the Flight to Captain F.W. Stent, who understood and spoke Arabic. The machines were well overdue for complete overhaul, their fabric was sagging and woodwork inclined to cracking. The mechanics were doing a wonderful job in keeping them going, for there were to be many more weeks of wartime flying ahead under these trying conditions.[9]

The first Battle of Gaza, which took place on 26 March 1917, was a costly failure for the British command.

According to one record, a list of No. 14 Squadron members, George Hynes, 1/AM, was in service in the Hejaz Campaign on 1 June 1917 as an Air Mechanic.[10]

Akaba, frequently mentioned by George as Aquaba, was still in the hands of the enemy until about a month later, 6 July 1917, when it was taken from the Turks by Lawrence and the tribesmen of the Hejaz Army and became a base for the Arab Northern Army and subsequently X Flight's principal landing ground during the rest of the war.

TWO LORDS A LEAPIN'

George's anecdotes certainly do bring aspects of the air war in the desert to life but, because he doesn't always give dates and locations, it has proved difficult to locate the stories in time and place. One such story is about two peers but one is left wondering about whom they actually were and what their association with the RFC was. Who was Lord Leighton? There was of course the famous artist who had no part in the war. Then there were two others, father and son, both of whom had military backgrounds and some association with the RFC.

George recounts:

> Lord Leighton's strict aristocratic ways created discord. He had a stern
> attitude towards Lord Selby, an Irish peer, and towards Lieutenant McLaren
> [MacLaren]. McLaren left us to reorganise a station at Alexandria and Selby
> left soon afterwards. One morning, when Selby was not flying over the canal,
> Lord Leighton followed Lord Selby into our wooden workshop.
>
> After Selby had bid us 'Good Morning' in his devil-may-care manner in
> display of comradeship that was common throughout the Royal Flying
> Corps, Leighton addressed Selby with 'Come on Selby. Go and do some
> flying!' Selby smiled back, 'Yes sir!' He then turned to us and came over to
> me.
>
> 'You can also enjoy a flip around with me if you wish.'
>
> I followed Lord Selby, started the Maurice Farman, giving it a flip.
>
> Selby ran it up and said, 'Engine OK! Jump in Hynes!' I didn't hesitate
> about climbing into the front cockpit and off we flew for a half-hour in the
> area of the Suez Canal on my first flight in Egypt.
>
> During his off duty hours, Selby used to delight in taking up his close
> companion Lieutenant Blake or me for a joyride. One morning as I was about
> to step into the machine, Lieutenant Blake dashed over, 'I'm coming with
> you this morning Selby!'
>
> I willingly stepped aside, as they were great friends. I swung the machine
> off to taxi into a position holding on to a wing. As Blake buckled himself in,
> Selby jokingly remarked, 'He would fiddle you out of the trip, Hynes!' He
> opened up the throttle and set off for his exercise.
>
> I returned to my job with Air Mechanic Johns, experimental work
> involving stripping the Lewis guns of their cumbersome radiators. About an
> hour later a call came in to say that the Maurice Farman had been forced to
> land in the European cemetery at Ismailiya!

MacLaren appears in a history of No. 14 Squadron where it is written, 'The First
BE to arrive (flown by Second Lieutenant Archie MacLaren of No. 14 Squadron)
dropped its blockbuster from no more than 100 ft. blowing an enemy aeroplane and
its attendant personnel on the ground to pieces.'[11]

JUNE 1917

CROSSLEY CAR TROUBLE

George recounts:

> Another incident during our operations at El Wejh involved Stafford and Air
> Mechanic Porter [6984 1/AM W. Porter, RFC] during a journey of two RFC
> Crossley tenders towards the Hejaz Railway taking a route never previously
> travelled. The Crossleys were the only transport available. I believe that the

Rolls Royce was far too heavy to attempt such a journey because of its extra weight of armour.

The cars always carried two sets of spare tyres for travel over those hot, dry sandy wastes filled with soft sinking sands. Then there were the miles and miles of rough ground strewn with sharp volcanic-looking pieces of rubble which tore at the walls of the tyres. The tenders carried big copper water containers to fill up the radiators at regular intervals. More space was taken up with acetylene-generating containers for the headlamps and bottles of life-saving water for the two occupants of each motor. Food, petrol and oil were necessary, as were other pieces of equipment including arms for defence. Heavy enough loads before taking into account packs of explosives or money to pay out tribes engaged in the fighting area.

Our machines naturally kept in contact with them when they could. On one occasion we were told that we had lost touch with one of those cars returning to El Wejh. For three days our four machines had been taking turns from dawn to nightfall to go out searching for the returning vehicle. Except for landing for a snack, Captain Stent was continually in the air without success.

Fortunately it was reported that a lone Arab with a camel had picked up the two occupants in a very bad condition and was bringing them into Wejh.

George continues:

It was a big relief to hear that they had been rescued from a nasty death. Thirst from which no person could survive after three days was a hazard in Southern Arabia. Stafford and Porter never did return to our camp. They were taken to Egypt on board ship for close medical attention as they were in a very low state.

The story we heard was that after completely running out of water they were about to commit themselves to death with their own revolvers. Fortunately a lone Arab with his camel had seen them and approached them at that critical time when they were about to follow that fatal decision. The Arab gave them a share of his small quantity of water, put them on his camel while he walked alongside to get them back to safety. They were so weak and feverish that they had become two human wrecks.

Help also reached the second Crossley which had also been waiting for water to return to us. Stafford's car had been found where it had been abandoned. Apparently its engine smelled like a dirty fish and chip shop for the two occupants in desperation had even put engine oil into the radiator to try and get back.

At age twenty-three, Stafford, then with the Royal Engineers, went out to China in 1900 with the 4th Balloon Section, later the Air Battalion, Royal Engineers, the foundation stone of the RFC. His RFC ID number was a very early one, No. 22! As a Sergeant he gained his Royal Aero Club Certificate 438 at the Central Flying

School at Upavon on 18 March 1913, the ninth NCO to do so. He served with No. 14 Squadron RFC in Egypt in 1914–15 and as a Sergeant Major was awarded the 1914–15 Star. There he was awarded the DCM and was commissioned. Stafford had served with C Flight all the way from 16 March to 31 July 1917 as the technical officer in charge of maintenance of the BE2c aeroplanes. He was awarded his MC on the same day as Capt. Henderson.

During his service in the Hejaz, Lieutenant Stafford and his air mechanic left Gayadah to return to Wejh. When they were found to be overdue a search was set up for them by air and land. Capt. Stent organised the air search and Lt Henderson the land search. Lt Henderson found the Crossley tender and with it a note signed by Lt Stafford. The note is in the copy of the Hejaz narrative in the research and the original is in the narrative of the Hejaz Expedition 1916–17.

Captain Thomas Henderson described the same incident:

> Owing to the roughness of the country between Wejh and Gayadah a tender and working party left on the 14th to prepare a suitable road for the advance of the Sherifial troops and the Egyptian force.[12]

Henderson continues:

> Several rough patches were successfully negotiated and ways clearly marked, making transport for the howitzers and armoured cars possible. A certain R.F.C. officer (Lieutenant W. G. Stafford) in charge of this tender and his working party, 6984 1/AM Porter W., very nearly lost their lives. He and his driver having run short of water owing to losing their way among the mountains were forced to subsist on their own urine to quench their thirsts for two days. They were eventually brought in by Bedouins who found them just in time. Having drank all the available water they had succeeded in running the tender using a mixture of grease and petrol in the radiator for engine cooling.[13]

A standard RFC procedure was followed to help in the search. Henderson issued the following:

PROPOSED PROGRAMME OF SEARCH PARTY (CAR).

1st day: Leave at EL WEJH AT 3 p.m.

Should arrive at ABU AJAJ in evening.

2nd day: Endeavour to pick up track of missing car.

If unsuccessful return to ABIJ AJAJ.

If there is time enough propose pushing on towards GAYADAH until I find Lt. Batting.

Probably spend night there.

3rd day: Return with Lt. Batting along tracks which he took going out.

4th day: Probably arrive back in EL WEJH

Note:-   The following code will be used between aeroplanes & ground party:-

Water required   <u>W</u>

Food required   <u>F</u>

Send another tender out   <u>Z</u>

Help urgently required   <u>H</u>

Land here   <u>L</u>

Require no help   <u>K</u>

To attract attention of aeroplanes a smoke ball will be thrown out from tender and then signal put out.

Search machines would greatly facilitate around search party's work if they kept car party supplied with information concerning ground reconnoitered from the air. Message bags therefore, containing this information, should be dropped on car party whenever possible.

The above signals will be used with a horizontal strip of <u>red</u> bunting underneath each letter to distinguish searching car from missing car.

If the sign 'H' is exposed and more than two cars are in evidence the search machine will return immediately to EL WEJH and bring out Medical Officer. Car party will endeavour to find best possible Landing Ground in the vicinity and put out the necessary signals.

The following signal will be put out when search is completed:-

[There followed a diagram of a large triangle above a strip of red bunting.]

EL WEJH. 22-6-17.
(signed) T. Henderson. Lt. for Capt. RFC.
Commanding 'C' Flight No. 14 Squadron,
Royal Flying Corps.

Rescuers found a note written by Stafford under a rock on or near the vehicle, 'We have no water. We have gone on to West into next Wadi going to keep West when possible. Hurry after us if you should see this. Cannot last long.' (Second Lieutenant W.G. Stafford was on No. 14 Squadron, C Flight, strength between 16 March, 1917 and 31 July 1917.)

George recounts an incident which probably occurred in late June 1917.

> Our small party comprising two Crossley tenders had left Gueira on that journey to the Madeba area to a large landing ground that Lawrence had previously selected. That landing ground was in the territory of a sheik, a former supporter of the Turks. Lawrence had personally won him over to our side persuading him to use his tribes against the Turks in the final push. Winning over such sheiks was possibly the most important action taken by Lawrence in enabling Allenby to make an all-out dash with his armoured cars, cavalry and aircraft and bringing about the collapse of the enemy.

Gueira was located on a red sandstone plain. Of an operation in which Lawrence took part with the Arabs, he commented:

> ...Howeitat, sheikh of the hill tribes, an old fox who had been balancing in his mind which side to take, was impressed by the victory and captured the Guweira [Gueira] garrison of a hundred and twenty men.[14]

George Hynes devoted many pages of his memoirs to the defence of Lawrence's reputation, which had been under assault by Aldington in his book, *Lawrence of Arabia: A Biographical Inquiry.* In later years, most historians came to agree with Aldington's account of the facts of Lawrence's life but certainly neither the general public nor George in 1955. The abuse aimed at Aldington from his critics was overwhelming and resulted in publishers refusing to print his works and bookstores refusing to stock them for lack of demand.[15]

Writing his thoughts down in 1961, George, and thinking like any other member of the general public of 1955, refused to accept Aldington's views. He writes:

> There is one person who recently passed away who could have hit hard at Aldington but man's laws in his status prevented him from speaking up. In all justice to him he was in at the finish at Derra; Lord Winterton because I know that he was a British gentleman and he respected Lawrence's advice on leadership as shown in my following story.

LORD WINTERTON COOKS BREAKFAST FOR LAWRENCE

George recounts:

> The Crossleys directed by Lawrence had to take a route across the railway out of the range of Turkish eyes, and cut in at night into Magdeba and settle on our landing ground for the night. [The Magdeba George mentions was probably Madeba, east of the Dead Sea.]
>
> The next morning, about dawn, breakfast was to be prepared for Lawrence, Lord Winterton and our party including Lt. Sefi, a pilot who had only just been posted to us. He was smaller than Lawrence. In fact he was the

smallest pilot officer I had ever set eyes on. I thought he must have been Armenian or Jewish. He could perhaps have been a Turk who had been sent through for some political reason to be in at the final, battle for while he was with us he never piloted any of our aircraft.

According to several X Flight weekly reports, Sefi had been very actively engaged in flying duties. Somehow he must have flown from landing grounds unattended by George who was more often than not in advance landing grounds administered from X Flight HQ in Akaba. After Captain V.D. Siddons had taken command of X Flight in place of Furness-Williams his reports mentioned Sefi more than once.

For example, in the X Flight Report for the week ending 20 July 1918 Siddons wrote, 'On the 20th.... Lt. Sefi tested a BE2A and on 27/7/18 Lt. Sefi was bombing the station at Mudwarra and machine gunning the enemy redoubts.'

On 28 June 1917 General Edmund Allenby left France to take command of Middle East operations in place of Murray.

George continues:

About June 1917, Winterton called out to one of our rigger mechanics who had only just arrived and been made corporal in charge of the fuelling and bombing up of Junor's aircraft.

'Wheeler what about breakfast this morning?' He spoke in the long haughty drawl of an English peer; but Lawrence interrupted in low polite tones.

'Yes! What about you Winterton making breakfast this morning? These men have had a rough time, getting here!'

Lord Winterton, who respected Lawrence's advice, replied in a cut glass accent, 'Good ideah! Give me the bacon, etcetrah, etcetrah' and set to while Corporal Wheeler and co settled down to light a fire of desert scrubs and twigs and commenced operations.

Winterton fried the bacon strips that must have been specially scrounged from somewhere because our flight never had such luxurious breakfasts when on advanced operations. He did his best but damn near burnt it all to a cinder! At least it was eaten and put us in good humour.

That incident involving Lord Winterton, unfamiliar with desert warfare, with Lawrence and we rankers was typical of the spirit of desert comradeship. Winterton came from a class we all looked up to and we had many such men fighting as volunteers in the Royal Flying Corps not sitting on their bottoms in Whitehall or in Cairo.

Lord Winterton had served with the Sussex Yeomanry at Gallipoli then spent most of his war service in the Middle East under Lawrence's command. During 1916 he commanded a company of the Imperial Camel Corps in operations, east of the Suez Canal against Bedouin tribesmen who supported the Turks.

Winterton and Lawrence kept in touch with each other after the war. In the early 1920s, at the request of the British government, he arranged for the Emir Feisal to become king of Iraq. Lawrence was party to those arrangements.

Lawrence also endeared himself to the rankers, sometimes taking their side against pompous people. Robert Graves wrote:

> So far as I know, he only once used the privileges of his rank for other than travelling. Once at a rest camp he stopped to watch a bullying officer bawling at two wretched privates, battle-weary men, who were passing on the far side of the barrack square: 'Come here, you two loungers! Take your hands out of your pockets! Why the hell didn't you salute me? Don't you know I'm a Major?' The poor fellows mumbled something. 'Now stand over there,' said the major, and let me see you march past and salute.' They obeyed and were walking off hurriedly when the major recalled them. 'Now come back and do it again properly.' They did it again. 'One moment, Major,' said a voice behind him; 'there is something you have forgotten.' The major wheeled round and saw a rather haggard-looking bareheaded boy in a tunic starred and crowned, on the shoulder, with badges of rank: Lawrence. The major saluted in confusion; the soldiers, happier now, were shuffling off but Lawrence beckoned them to stop. 'The thing that you have forgotten, Major,' Lawrence went on gently, 'is that in this army the salute is paid not to the man but to the rank, and the officer saluted is ordered by the King, whom he represents, to return the salute. But of course you know that.' The major was speechless. 'You will therefore salute those men,' said Lawrence, 'whose salutes just now you failed to return.' The major saluted, choking with rage. But the merciless Lawrence continued: 'Major, those private soldiers saluted you twice. You will therefore return their salutes a second time.' And the major had to obey.[16]

That incident, probably not reported elsewhere, accords well with Lawrence's use of the mischievous 'put down' such as another described by Robert Graves in *Lawrence and the Arabs*.

> Early in his career in Cairo, Lawrence felt so plagued by useless generals that he set about making himself so obnoxious that the General Staff would get rid of him. One day the chief of staff rang him and asked, 'Is that Captain Lawrence? Where exactly is the Turkish Forty-First Division now stationed?' Lawrence said, 'At So-and-So near Aleppo. The 131st, 132nd, 133rd regiments compose it. They are quartered in the villages So-and-So, So-and-So, and So-and-So.'
> 'Have you those villages marked on the map?'
> 'Yes.'
> 'Have you noted them yet on the Dislocation map?'
> 'No.'

23

'Why not?'

'Because they are better in my head until I can check the information.'

'Yes, but you can't send your head along to Ismailia every time.'(Ismailia was a long way from Cairo.)

'I wish to goodness I could,' said Lawrence, and rang off.'

It was decided to get rid of him![17]

George gave his opinion of Murray.

> On our move towards Gaza, Murray had commanded that advance from Cairo but as a professional military commander he had not fully realised the value of the air support. When I was there in Arabia I was annoyed by lackadaisical attitudes by the high command but after reading Philby's book I have since developed a certain sympathy for Murray because as a general, he had to put up with conflicting opinions of politicians and ignorant ministers who were totally ignorant of military strategies. General Murray had to obey their instructions and commands.

According to Henderson who was with C Flight the fourth raid on El Ula was carried out by three machines (4488, flown by Lt Henderson, 5241 flown by 2/Lt V.D. Siddons and 4478 flown by Lt W.L. Fenwick) on 16 July 1917. This time the water tower was hit and much material damage done.

EL WEJH DROME, SUMMER 1917

George continues:

> I returned to El Wejh, my second time back to Arabia, to a much different type of warfare. At El Wejh I had soon settled down having met some of my pals from the original 14 Squadron: Wheeler, Pounds, Caldwell, Shaw, New, Mercer, Stokes and others along with four conscientious objectors. The objectors were employed on general duties blending in with the team under the command of Captain Stent, a man who was game for anything where aerial activity was concerned.

The Flight started out with a handful of BE12 aircraft carrying out aerial reconnaissance on behalf of the irregular Sherifian ground forces and Captain Lawrence himself. Although the Flight's principal task lay in aerial photography and reconnaissance every opportunity was taken to bomb and strafe the enemy, especially the railway security parties, those along the lines and in the stations. According to most pilots the BE12 was utterly incapable of combat but nevertheless was occasionally used in aerial fights. Fortunately for the Flight, it did get a couple of two-seater BE2e machines, which flew at 70 mph, and a single-seater DH2 'pusher'(engine behind the pilot) working out of Akaba.

Lawrence remembered El Wejh and a journey in an RFC machine.

She took two days to reach Wejh. Feisal, with Joyce, Newcombe, and all the army, was at Jeida, one hundred miles inland. Stent, who had succeeded Ross in command of the Arabian flight, sent me up by air; so we crossed comfortably at sixty miles an hour the hills learned toilsomely on camel-back.[18]

Captain T. Henderson of No. 14 Squadron also remembered Wejh. According to him, after a raid on El Ula on 16 July 1917, the next day a severe sandstorm hit C Flight's camp after which the machines flew into Wejh and after being declared unserviceable were dismantled and packed into cases ready for shipment to Egypt. Then, 'On July 31st loading of all machines and stores on to the steamer *El Kahirta* was completed whereupon it steamed out to H.M.S. *Dufferin*, transferred everything over on the 1st August and proceeded to Egypt.'[19]

AIRCRAFT AND EQUIPMENT PUT ON BOARD HMS DUFFERIN

George who must have been with C Flight in El Wejh at that time, before the formation of X, described the move.

> We suddenly got orders to pack up, to strip hangars and to dismantle machines, to put them in their cases with the rest of the equipment for storage on board HMS *Dufferin*. The cases were so large they had to be slung on the life boat davits over the side of the ship.
>
> We were on our way to Suez in temperatures of over a hundred degrees, steaming up the Red Sea. We were hailed by HMS *Hardinge* which moved in so that she could be lashed to the starboard side of our ship for her to receive all our equipment.
>
> The naval crew and we in the RFC worked in relief parties to unload our ship and to transfer all our gear into the *Hardinge*. We worked half hour shifts, first on deck then in the hold as it was far too hot to stay down in the hold where the sweat poured off us and we drank large quantities of lime juice with water with a little rum during the night.
>
> It was hard work and sweating with our shirt off and the winches in constant use until daybreak the next morning and the sea was as calm as a pond not a breeze with a good job done and then completed our journey to Suez. Looking back I feel proud of that co-operation between the two services on that occasion when the task was completed with a will and without any grumbling.
>
> We arrived at Suez and in a couple of days at the drome. Along with five others I was drafted up to Sinai by train from Kantara. For a short while we worked once again on our very first landing ground, the one we had previously used on our first advance across the canal. We settled down to receive and attend to four machines the next morning. They were to be used in the bombing operations across Sinai to support Lawrence in his surprise

attack on that Turks at Ma'an and Abu al Lissal before going on to capture Aquaba [Akaba].

The Turks had a flying school at Ma'an, a place which is about 4,000 feet above sea level. At that height during very hot periods of the day the air density is so low that attempted aircraft take-offs were really very hazardous.

> That was when our southern X Flight became a small party in Aquaba while the remaining personnel returned to No. 14 Squadron in Gaza. Our party consisting of three pilots and eight ground crew continued operating with Lawrence out of Wegh. [Wejh or Wegh lies about 240 miles south of Akaba on the eastern shore of the Red Sea.]
>
> We put up our canvas hangars, two marquees and a couple of bell tents and using the two tenders and our expanding trailers we brought our supplies from the ship. Those supplies had been transported from ship to a jetty built by the crew of HMS *Euryalus* to enable Arab dhows to come closer to the shore. A blue painted board had been placed on a pole near the jetty with the inscription, 'HMS *Euryalus* finished this jetty because Solomon had not finished it.' Or words to that effect. Signed at the bottom: 'The crew of the HMS *Euryalus*, 1917.' [HMS *Euryalus* started service in Suez in February 1915 but was sold for scrap in 1920!]

Early in his memoirs George made some observations about the enemy.

> We had beaten the Turks after the defeats on the Dardanelles. The first defeat was at Ismailiya, and there were no French troops in that battle, and none on the Sinai Peninsular [sic] to Gaza, when we had to retard the advance. The fact was that a couple of weeks after the Ismailiya success, many British troops including Australians were drafted out to France. I was surprised when I saw the first French soldiers, the Foreign Legion battalions, boarding railway coaches at Kantara, in July 1917 on which we travelled to Mustabig our first landing ground in Sinai ready to help Lawrence in Quintilla [Kuntilla].

George continued with:

> They were the first French I ever saw. The next French I saw was when a four gun battery were involved in firing practice with seventy fives, in September 1918, near the sloping escarpment of the hills of Wadi Araba. Such weapons were too heavy to be transported for action at Ma'an and Mudowwara.
>
> Our little party of six had also boarded that same train to Kilo 143, a few miles south of El Arian, to be ready to receive our four machines that we had taken from El Wejh and assembled at Suez to enable our pilots to operate across Sinai to Quintilla [Kuntilla], to assist Lawrence and his Army to clear the way and capture Aquaba.

Much to the astonishment of the top brass in Cairo, Lawrence and his Arabs took Akaba on 6 July 1917 and it became the base for the Arab Northern Army and the principal landing ground for X Flight throughout the rest of the conflict.

ANOTHER TEMPORARY AIRFIELD IN EL ARISH

George continues:

> Our four aircraft had operated for about six days from our temporary ground south of the El Arish [on the coast of Palestine] across to Quintilla. A heavy attack was mounted on Abu el Lissal. We then returned to Suez and picked up our kit to board ship to Aquaba arriving there shortly after Lawrence's army took it. Our camp was soon laid out in the Wadi Araba [north-east of Akaba] and our machines flew over from the Suez.

AN EGYPTIAN MURDER CASE

George was suitably horrified by the murder of an Egyptian soldier by his own colleagues when on guard duty on detachment with the RFC.

> We also had a very disturbing case of murder at El Wejh in the Egyptian battalion. An incident that could have brought dissension in Lawrence's alliances among the tribes and interruption in our operations. An Egyptian sergeant and three privates had been doing guard duty at night on our landing ground. The next morning one of the privates had been found brutally murdered while on sentry duty. He had been shot and a tent peg had been driven through him, right through his body into the sand. The top of a copper water container had been placed on top of him and an attempt had been made to suggest an Arab had committed the murder.
>
> After about two weeks of close confinement under arrest in a tent, and a careful investigation, the sergeant in charge of the guard and two privates were found guilty of murder. An examination of their rifles proved that one of them had killed his companion. The murdered man had won some gold while gambling so they stole it back from him. One of his companions had carried out the murder with the co-operation of the sergeant in charge and his other two sentries.
>
> The killers had tried to make it look as if an Arab had committed the murder. If such an accusation had reached the ears of the Arabs it would have caused a great deal of trouble in Wegh where we were not really accepted by the Arabs as reliable partners. The three were sentenced to death.
>
> An execution was carried out in the sand dunes just outside our camp in the presence of the whole Egyptian battalion. The accused sat on a bench by an open grave where they were shot by firing squad at about five thirty on a bright sunny morning. It was very unpleasant.

THE MEDICAL OFFICER

George recounts:

> Throughout our service, we were constantly cared for by having large weekly doses of quinine and inoculations to keep us fit. Our Medical Officer, Marshall, had a fondness for the needle and he did his work well keeping us free from sickness.

Marshall appears in a list of attached officers, 'The following officers should be detailed by the O.C. troops, Northern Hejaz, to accompany the column from Akaba: Political Officer for liaison with Arabs: Major Marshall, M.C., R.A.M.C. (in addition to duties as M.O.).[20]

AUGUST 1917

George continues:

> Within a couple of days, the landing ground was complete, the machines serviced and test flights were carried out. The cookhouse or 'make-up' consisted of a few stones supporting iron bars outside our tents. We took turns at cooking. Each man got his rations in his personal mess tin. The bread ration was distributed by the Royal Army Service Corps attachment from the ship's bakery on HMS *Humber*. We received half a loaf a day, just under a pound in weight, along with a daily ration of a couple of army-type 'dog biscuits'.

HMS *Humber* had previously been launched for the Brazilian Navy in 1913 as the *Javary*. It was bought by the Royal Navy in 1914 and later sold for use as a crane ship in 1920. She served in the eastern Mediterranean as a guardship at Akaba from August 1917 to February 1918.

George again:

> Radio communication at Aquaba was by HMS *Humber*, the Monitor, with the Naval Command and no field service except the small radio set in our Flight and such if used by both was in secret code and Lawrence made it his business to deliver important matters relating to operations and such matters of secrecy to those concerned in person.
>
> A typical daily menu consisted of:
>
> Breakfast; boiled oatmeal, tinned milk (if any available), a rasher of bacon (again, if any available), tea in our enamel mugs.
>
> Dinner; meat (if available!) or bully beef stew with a little potato
>
> Afters; boiled rice with a little Ideal tinned milk or sugar content [not plentiful] and perhaps a spoonful of 'Possy', that is jam. [The word 'possy'

meaning jam, was in general use during World War One both in the trenches and in Blighty.]

Tea; last meal of the day; a cup of tea, the remainder of the bread ration, a small piece of cheese [if available] a portion of butter and a spoonful of jam and make the best of it till next morning!

Supper; at leisure at night, a couple of dog biscuits to sit in our candle lit hangars or to play cards to pass the time away. Our cigarette ration was then about 50 per week and two books of matches, de-rationed later.

The first brick cook-house in Akaba was built by a Royal Engineers working party on 23 March 1918.

We had three other pilots and 'ground pilot' who was at one time, our Warrant Officer, Stafford, a technical engineer for the squadron. He had served with the Royal Engineers Balloon Unit. The two RFC Crossleys were in his charge. They were used for transporting patrols and supplies to our forward landing grounds and further afield co-operating with Feisal, Ali and Abdulla's forces when attacking Medina and Mecca.

Stafford had done his flying training in Farmans aircraft when he was one of Trenchard's first pilots. The Farmans was the training kite when the war broke out and it remained in use throughout 1915 until the Avro and the BE2C Royal Aircraft Factory design came off the lines.

His [Stafford's] flying certificate had very early number issued at about the same time as that of Dismore who finished his career as a pilot in the Imperial Air Service after the war.

Captain F.W. Stent, was posted to 14 Sqn RFC in March 1917. Later, he took over from Major Ross D.S.O. as Officer Commanding 'C' Flight in the Hejaz. At the end of the Hejaz campaign, probably on 2 May 1917 until 31 July, 1917, he took command of the Special Duty Flight and 'X' Flight of 14 Sqn, probably in September, until the end of October. The Flight's operational support was decided by Lt. Colonel P.C. Joyce who commanded the British forces of the Northern Army.

THE TIN LIZZY (POSSIBLY LATE 1917)

George recounts:

There were also times of high humour at El Wejh. For example, headquarters in Cairo had presented a 'Tin Lizzie', a T Ford car, as a present to Hussein who passed it on to Feisal but it was no use to him either in driving over desert wastes. It did however frequently arrive at our camp driven by a big black Sudanese man about six feet four inches tall! Judging from his broad grin showing a gleaming set of teeth he enjoyed his master's car very much indeed. He never ever had a passenger while he amused himself driving about the desert in the Lizzy.

One day Captain Stent came up to Jimmy Caldwell to have the car's punctured tyre made serviceable. 'Jimmy there's no spare tyre for this car. They have overlooked the matter of spares. Can you do anything about it?'

Jimmy thought hard about it and suggested that the only thing that could be done was to get some hay or straw and pack the outer tyre casings. The idea gave us a good laugh but it was the only practical solution. Stent replied with, 'Good for you Jim. That should suit him nicely. What's more they will do better over the sandy ground and stand continual abuse. That's settled. Please do your best!' He chuckled as he walked away.

Jimmy found some straw, probably in the village, and stuffed the tyres as hard as he could. Funnier still, the Sudanese, drove happily away with bits of straw sticking out of the rims of the tyres.

The next time I saw Lizzy was when we were running across Desi mud flat, just before Christmas on our way, in a Crossley, to our aircraft parking place to bomb up. He joined us in a race across the flat. We lost sight of it but saw it later toppled over on its side while going over a three-foot high sand dune. We got it back onto its wheels and it 'steamed' off again after the driver had filled the radiator it having lost some water in the tip over.

It was likely that the armoured cars section had regularly maintained the Lizzie which could only be used for short distances convenient to Gueira.

The Sudanese man was probably one of Feisal's Freedmen, former slaves who had been granted their freedom.

Stent went on to command No. 111 Squadron in Palestine, as a Major, until the end of hostilities. According to Henderson's account cited in Roger Bragger's internet site. Having settled in at Wejh, the future offensive was to be entirely against the Hejaz Railway. It being April, the weather was much better, but the heat was much greater and this was badly affecting the machines' engine cylinders, which were now prone to cracking – a constant problem in the weeks to come.

GEORGE ON HORSES AND THE FORMATION OF X FLIGHT

Air Mechanic George spent his war repairing and maintaining some second rate aircraft which X Flight had to put up with during its secret operations in the desert wastes. Of course he was devoted to engineering and took pride in his skills with those early flying machines but he was also fascinated by the horses and camels which were used so skilfully by the Arabs who lived in those deserts.

Of the horses he wrote:

During my boyhood days at about the age of twelve I used to go the stables of carriage contractors to take a shire horse out for exercise on a Sunday morning and bank holidays after the carter had cleaned and fed his horse.

Then he wrote:

> There was a thrill riding such animals. In fact I had to satisfy my longing for a ride by arranging pleasure beach horses into an organised race, one day on my firm's annual outing. It cost us each a shilling a ride in an all out race with my fellow companions while the owner shouted at us for urging them to run faster than they had ever run before.

He continued:

> When I was a member of our Flight in Arabia I felt I would have liked to have been able to join Lawrence with his roaming Arabs when I was close to him on occasions. I had ridden camels on Sinai to collect food rations before the railway had reached us and when possible I would steal a ride on one of the six Arab horses that we had in case of having to go to the aid of a downed machine escaping capture by the Turks.

George went on to say that shortly after the Flight had been set up with a small number of officers and mechanics, he borrowed three Arab horses to collect food rations from the village of Akaba. By then he had learned that travel by camel and horse was often a much better option than travel in mechanised vehicles.

> On duty, on special occasions, along with my pal Air Mechanic Pendrons, we rode camels to pick up the Squadrons' rations from the Royal Army Service food dump at the rear of our advancing army in the Sinai. For a couple of weeks with a caravan of twelve camels we went through See Saw rides throughout the journeys until the 'ships of the desert' got down on their knees. I felt very sorry for our wounded who had to be conveyed on camels' backs; one stretcher slung on each side of a camel's hump, moving about two feet up and down. More uncomfortable than a ship in the Bay of Biscay.

George went on to describe a curious moment he witnessed when travelling in the Flight's most popular conveyance, the Crossley tender.

> Just after we arrived at Aquaba, I was travelling with one of our Crossleys with three other mechanics and the driver, we stopped near a large rock about fifty feet high. One side was like a vertical wall. We had stopped to top up the radiator as it had been steaming in the intense heat. We were surprised to see a lone Arab hitting the side of the hill with rapid strokes. Being curious, we went over to him and asked him what he was doing. He turned to us and opened a small piece of goatskin, showing us a white paste and offered it to us to taste. We tried a very minute portion on our fingers; each in turn, tasted it, and then he pointed down indicating that it was milk from a goat. He then closed the bag and showed us his method of making cheese. It was about as much that would cover two slices of our British made loaf. Continuing on our journey we got stuck in some very soft deep sand that compelled us to get it out by putting desert scrubs under the wheels and pushing the tender to firmer ground close to Rhumm. We came across a very large block of

granite-like stone almost cubic that was about two hundred and twenty five cubic feet and about forty tons in weight. [Rhumm or Rumm is about 20 miles from Akaba. The Wadi Rumm is a valley cutting through sandstone and granite rock – the largest wadi in Jordan. In ancient Aramaic, the word Rum means high.]

This huge block lay on the scrub near Rhumm but there were no hills nearby. It looks as if it had just been dropped there. We wondered how it ever got there. We thought about the three mile wide Wadi Araba, bordered by hills; the Wadi Ithm with its open gateway of four foot high walls; the seven miles wide Desi mudflat. What was even more fascinating was the desert moon seen as we sat outside our tent late at night. It rose over the horizon at the extreme end of the mudflat, moving quickly and four times larger than back home. It lit up everything in a silvery glow almost as bright as day. We five mechanics just sat in wonder. Perhaps the Turkish patrols out in the wilderness of the Nagao hills were filled with the same wonderment. [The Wadi Ithm is near Kethira just north-west of Akaba whereas the Wadi Araba goes north to the Dead Sea and beyond.]

GEORGE TAKES HIGH TEA WITH A TURK

George recounts:

There were no market stalls or means of purchasing anything in Aquaba except on two occasions for me when I went to the jetty a couple of times. A young Turk always made it his business to invite me to join him in a pot of tea in an Arab's shack. He was my Turkish friend on board the ship.

He was a decent type of about my own age who was one of about 100 Turkish prisoners of war who had travelled with us on the ship to join Feisal's army. He wore light drill clothing originally with a red Turkish head fez which he discarded when we arrived at Aquaba after which he wore Arab head dress and khaki woollen material. Jafen Pasha came aboard with other Turks who swore allegiance. The red fez was thrown overboard into the Gulf waters.

During another journey, we became friends so Malik and I had many a chat. He told me he was a schoolteacher who spoke good English. I was also shown some of his handiwork made with coloured beads supplied to him in camp. His craftwork was unique so I bought some at very reasonable prices. There were two pieces that particularly attracted me so I offered to buy one.

Malik would not part with them because he had made them to present to the Emir Feisal. They were sashes made in four colours with diamond shaped designs on the back. On the white underside, running the full length in black letters in English was worked, 'Made by a Turkish prisoner of war, 1917'.

On the last day Malik came to me saying, 'Take one of these as a present and please give the other one to Feisal.' I offered to pay for them.

'No you must have it from me!'

Still I gave him some packets of cigs and told him I would be vexed if he did not accept something. He then accepted ten shillings but he made me take two small ladies' 'Dorothy' bags both in black beads with a large Maltese crosses on each.

I very seldom got down to the village for most of my time was spent in advance positions at Mudowarra and Gueira. When I did manage to get to the village, Malik and I always have had a friendly pot of tea.

He used to take me to the Arab shack where there was a little table in one corner with a copper tea urn for boiling water. I supposed it was from the loot of the wrecked trains and was being made good use of there as we enjoyed our pot of tea, the Arab way with a glass of cool water. No milk was used in the tea but there was plenty of sugar.

There was no furniture in the shack, just a bare earthen floor. Malik and I would simply sit on a small carpet with the teapot, two cups and two glasses of water. There might also be about four Arabs there smoking hookers [hookahs] and filling the atmosphere with that aromatic smell that blends with the Arab and his surroundings. The smoking is associated with contentment, relaxation and friendship.

Such were the close relationships between Arabs, Turkish co partners and the British in Aquaba. All built up in such a short time, less than twelve months due to Lawrence. There was only one guardship there, HMS *Humber*, a monitor ship communicating with HQ by wireless.

Occasionally George compared the characters of Arabs and Egyptians, saying that the latter were more likely to practise dishonesty. He gives an example.

An Egyptian labourer who had been stationed in Aquaba Drome as a servant asked me to lend him my Big Ben watch when I was about to move to Decie preparing attacks on Mudwarra. One of his jobs was to wake an NCO [Duty NCO probably] at 4 a.m. each morning. I lent it to him. When I returned I asked for its return but the man said he had sold it to an Arab. The Egyptian, like a naughty boy who did not realise his stealing was wrong, brought back the watch case and its mechanism in pieces. He had taken it to pieces to show the Arab what was inside it.

A PLOT TO BLOW UP THE AKABA FORT

George recounts:

The Aquaba [Akaba] Arabs told us that an attempt was to be made to destroy the Arab fort in the village. Following that an attempt would be made rescue an enemy pilot.

That loyal comradeship brought us news of an enemy plot to blow up the old fort used to store explosives and captured weapons just near the landing

33

jetty in Aquaba. [Probably the 12th century, Crusader fortress of Helim.]

The story was that a plot had been hatched by some of the Turkish officers who had joined the Arab army. Their plot was disclosed by one of the Turks, possibly to Jaffa Pasha Feisal or to Colonel Joyce who had become the base commander.

We learned later that the Emir Feisal had held a court martial in the Arab manner and the plotters were sentenced to be shot and no doubt they were.

SOME OBSERVATIONS BY GEORGE ABOUT TURKS

Although in later years George came to realise how the politicians had let down his great hero, Lawrence, he retained a naïve belief in British political virtue. The following paragraph refers:

It must be known that the British in the field of Battle in the Middle East, had not gone to steal Turkish or Arab property, but to fight for the freedom of her allies in all areas. The proof is here; when we were advancing on Sinai, our pilots were carrying thousands of leaflets printed in Egyptian-size newspaper in three languages requesting the Turks to pack in, and to words of the like; 'We do not want to fight you, we are fighting the Germans. Give in now as friends. Here is the evidence of the care and attention we are giving to your men in our hands.' This evidence was shown in the illustrated pictures of Turkish prisoners of war in comfortable quarters in Cairo, and the prisoners making use of their skills and craftsmanship.

He continues with:

Further proof of those comforts was that prisoners were given cigarettes leaving us short in our cigarette rations, especially in Arabia. Our food rations had also been cut down to the meanest levels as were clothing replacements. In one period we never had a ration of cigs for over four months.

We had been told that due to cigarettes being issued to the Turks, there was a shortage. Our only pleasure in off-duty hours during the dark nights was reduced to no more than lying on our makeshift beds.

Our officers and men did not hate the Turks in battle, as those boys were good fighters but we overlooked the fact that the Arabian warriors were fighting a Turkish enemy who had oppressed them for centuries. The Arabian native was a much cleaner type, loyal as a friend in battle, and a clean fighter after centuries of desert life. Hatred between Turks and Arabs was mutual especially as the Turks had been given freedom to treat Arabs like animals showing no mercy raping and butchering village inhabitants.

September 1917

Lawrence wrote:

> Accordingly I planned to march five hundred regular mounted infantry, the battery of French quick-firing .65 mountain-guns, proportionate machine guns, two armoured cars, sappers, camel scouts and two aeroplanes to Azrak where their concentration must be complete by September the thirteenth. On the sixteenth we would envelop Deraa, and cut its railways.[21]

Two X Flight machines flew over Qasr el Azraq and then looked at a railway at Derra. No big air attack could be made so Lawrence concentrated on cutting railway lines.

On September 12, X Flight's Bristol shot down an enemy two-seater but was very badly damaged and had to go to Palestine for repair.

October 1917

> There's beauty in the rocky wastes (As long as the prop. goes round)[22]

George continues:

> Captain Furness-Williams, our new commanding officer, had arrived in October 1917. Another two machines, Martinsydes, had been sent over. Just after our midday meal I was detailed to fly on to Decie with Lieutenant Junor. We set off but as we were flying over Rhum [about 30 miles east of Akaba] and I was peering over the cockpit, I suddenly felt I was going to be sick.
>
> To prevent me being sick all over the inside of the cockpit, I pulled off my head dress and vomited into it stooping low in the cockpit to prevent the pilot, who was sitting behind me, from getting it in his slipstream. I threw the bundle overboard as we flew over Rhum.
>
> That was the first time I had ever been sick and I hated having to throw away that woven silk cloth that I had been able to roll up and put in my pocket when working in the sun.
>
> I am sure that the immediate cause was my having to inhale the oil fumes from the engine crank breathers which let out the hot vapours. That and the Maconochie ration together had done the damage. After a couple of weeks at Decie and a return to Aquaba, I suffered with pains in my gums and finally a swollen face which resulted in a trip to Suez for a treatment in the latter part of November.
>
> In Decie, we slept in bell tents during the cold nights with only two blankets covered by army greatcoats. In the matter of personal comforts there we had plenty of water for drinking and washing because it was brought to us in Crossley tenders. Our clothes were kept free from vermin by swilling them in petrol. Arabs on the move took only sufficient water and food to keep them alive washing only when they arrived in villages.

OPERATING FROM DECIE

George recalls:

> We became very busy operating from Decie. Our aircraft would return to Aquaba before dusk while Lawrence was busy organising and taking part in train wrecking and sometimes being taken by our aircraft to Palestine and Egypt.
>
> It was about October when we had received word that some additional ground crew had arrived on a ship at Aquaba. A few of them had refused to be inoculated and so could not land. This problem was solved and we had another 20 men to be trained and to strengthen our party.
>
> The Martinsydes had done much to keep the enemy aircraft confined to a safe distance, only venturing towards Aquaba at about eight to ten thousand feet. The Turks seemed to be more active on the Palestine front. Our original B.E.2cs were in use until Captain Furness-Williams taking over in October 1917 improved our Flight of four, 4 year old B.E.2cs to B.E.12s, Martinsydes and Nieuport Scouts.

The name Martinsyde was given to aircraft produced by H.P. Martin and George Handasyde, well known as Martin & Handasyde. Post war, in December 1919, a Martinsyde flown by a Captain C.E. Howell, left London in a race to Australia. He was delayed by bad weather although he had left England in the hope of arriving first.

There were various versions of the Nieuport French biplane fighter, the Nieuports 11 and 17, for example. The Nieuport 17 entered service with the RFC in the summer of 1916, becoming very popular with fighter pilots for its agility and rate of climb. The early overwing Lewis gun was later replaced by a synchronised Vickers.

AN ATTACK BY AN ENEMY AIRCRAFT

The attack described here by George Hynes must have been made on Akaba where there were more facilities for the personnel.

> One afternoon, following the first enemy bomb raid at about 1030 at night, I had returned from the bottom of our drome with a pal who had worked with me on the maintenance of the Lewis guns. We had been to the YMCA canteen, a very large marquee, where our troops could get a backshee [buckshee] cup of cocoa and where they could buy biscuits cigs and chocolate.
>
> I had a Lewis gun fitted on a wooden prop, four inches square, ready for any approaching raiders. Whoever was on the gun was instructed to give three volleys warning of any night attack to rouse all for miles round. Enemy aircraft would first release bombs at the railway siding going after the railhead. The warning shots would give the hospital time to prepare. The

enemy had become rather ruthless a few days before, shelling a field hospital from Samson's Ridge. Following that our machines had gone into action at once and destroyed the battery of four guns.

I returned to the camp and entered my tent where my mate was in his ground bed. He told me an early reconnaissance aircraft would have to be made ready for the early morning flight at dawn, about four fifteen. I told him not to bother.

Lewis guns were to be taken out of their boxes where we kept them after each gun had been cleaned and tested after every flight. They were placed in their cases to prevent sand particles getting into any of the mechanism causing stoppages. I placed the first gun into its mounting in an aircraft along with four drums of ammo and returned to the bell tent alongside our canvas hangars to get a second gun.

I was about to enter when I heard a swishing sound as if an enemy machine was gliding in directly from the sea over the Arab village so I ran to the gun mounted on the wooden prop and blasted off three volleys.

Bombs were dropped in a line over our hangars and I saw the attacker pass just ahead of the only white cloud overhead. It was very difficult to see machines at night but I knew that one was near the cloud so I took that as my target passed over. Outside the hangar, the gun raised from chest level I gave him a rally.

Meanwhile then the gun outside the officers' quarters on the other side of the drome had been manned and it followed up with a volley just before the enemy reached B Flight hangars. His first bombs had damaged a new Martinsyde with a burst of ammo. I moved my position stopping a few yards to the rear of the hangar amongst small sand mounds enclosed by the kind of scrub seen everywhere in the Middle East.

As I moved I heard another enemy machine gliding in towards us, at a low altitude, 80 ft., so I gave another burst as it approached in the wake of the first raider. There were four explosions nearby and I was blasted with sand. The raider's bombs had fallen short of our hangars. They had dropped across the narrow wadi on lower ground close to A Flight hangars.

Our machines bombed all day and at the end of the day another plan was put into operation to lead the enemy into new a trap giving the enemy aircraft a real trouncing. At the end of the day we received orders to load up with bombs and refuel all aircraft for them to take off before dusk. We were to select a landing ground away from Gaza ready to follow the enemy back to their own drome.

Our intelligence service was doing excellent work. Information about enemy positions and intentions reached us quickly. Now the word from the enemies' area was that there would be two raids tonight. The first raid at about ten thirty when the moon appeared over the top of the Gaza Hills. Another raid would follow at about two o' clock in a full moonlight attack.

The report was correct and a barrage of gunfire opened up in the hills. The noise drowned out the sound of approaching raiders. As our drome was raided we just lay down flat in our hangars as we never did build dugouts. We took our chances in the flying shrapnel. The machines escaped damage.

Our machines actually took to the air during that raid and timing their take off to follow the enemy machines back to their drome. Each of our machines followed the enemy aircraft inland dropping their bombs on the enemy. The enemy machines returned after reloading with fuel and bombs at two o' clock but our aircraft repeated their own follow up.

All day we continued our bombing missions and during the whole time only one enemy aircraft came over our lines at about eight thousand feet. Our only anti-aircraft defence consisted of two old Boer War pom poms which could not do any damage to the attacker but our fighters took off after him forcing him to take a dive into his own territory. Our aircraft continued the troop support work.

Our machines kept up the daily activity but the enemy made another raid on four aircraft about during the next night. Seeing that our aircraft were away I decided to go with air mechanic Featherstone visiting from B Flight to the YMCA tent for a cup of cocoa as we never received any food after our six o' clock evening meal until the next morning.

Having had our cup of cocoa and a packet of biscuits and we'd decided to return to our quarters. However some of the chaps in the canteen told us that Allenby was shaking things up for more support for the front line troops and we now had a field cinema. The cinema was operated in a very long marquee. Featherstone and I went in and joined the boys who were already watching a silent picture of Charlie Chaplin. Another film being shown of scenes in Blighty had pictures of a Tommy rowing a boat with his lady friend reclining in the stern wearing a nice white dress. The boys in the cinema tent showed their appreciation with cries of, 'Oh boy, what a peach! Lucky dog!' but all that came to a stop when we heard three volleys from the drome followed by four explosions. Everyone rushed out to take cover.

Featherstone shouted, 'Come on George, this place is a real target! Dive under these railway trucks.' The trucks were close to the marquee so we were able to dive under them just as the first machine flew all over the drome selecting our wagons for his remaining four bombs. There were only three machines in this raid and each made the wagons their target and on their return machine-gunning our troops as they flew back to their own lines.

The four bombs fell down the side of the embankment where field hospital tents were parked. One bomb fell into a small marquee setting it on fire with flames which lit up the whole area. Unfortunately it turned out to be the dispensary filled with inflammable spirits and chemicals used by the RAMC. Four RAMC men had been killed there.

During that raid I felt as if a mule had kicked me in my left leg. As soon as the last raider left off his attempt to destroy the wagons we both crawled from under our shelter and made our way back to camp. After that blow in my leg I was surprised to find that when I stood on my feet my legs felt OK. Featherstone who had also been hit in the back told me that after feeling the blow he examined his great coat and found a tear in it although he was uninjured.

I could walk and never troubled to look at my left leg until I pulled off my drill slacks to bed down on the ground sheet and I then found a small shrapnel tear at the back of my leg at the knee joint but it was so small that I never bothered to report it. Many years afterwards I realised how foolish I had been to ignore it because although small it had travelled through my body ending up in my bowel! That was discovered after I had suffered a sudden pain which resulted in me driving across a level crossing into the arms of the law and a ten shilling fine. I then had a major operation to remove the shrapnel.

It dawned on me that using my gun near the hangar had helped the second raider who would have used the tracer bullets as a guide to his target. I stopped firing and ceased further use of the gun but the other gun at the officers' quarters continued firing.

It turned out that the only damage was to the Martinsyde Scout and the canvas hangar. Both had been perforated with shrapnel from the first bombs. The Martinsyde could not be used in the next air operations.

The raiders dropped their remaining loads on the railway siding and after turning towards Beersheba dropped a few on our troop encampments without causing any serious damage.

Captain Freeman, our flight commander, dashed over to see if any serious damage had been done and at his orders we ran out a Sopwith Pup in which he followed the raiders to their base in Beersheba returning a few hours later with the words, 'Settle yourselves down there will be no more raiders tonight. All machines will be leaving at dawn loaded with bombs.'

The enemy thought they had given us a nasty crack and they realised that they may expect a return attack which we made the next day along with the Australian Squadron. The enemy dump and drome at Beersheba received our bombs at the rate of about 40 to one of theirs dropped on us.

The Sopwith Pup was a single-seater biplane fighter aircraft much more useful to Captain Freeman in pursuit than any BE2c could ever have been. This plane made by the Sopwith Aviation Company was officially called the Sopwith Scout. The nickname arose because pilots spoke of it as being the 'pup' of the larger two-seater Sopwith Strutter. Although the authorities thought the nickname to be undignified it gave rise to the practice of giving the names of mammals or birds, (for example, Camel, Dolphin, Snipe) to subsequent models.

George continues:

> At another time after a busy couple of days of raiding operations, rumours were afloat that an army search party had entered an Arab village and found a couple of machine guns and a pile of ammunition. Despite that we were receiving regular information, Sherifial Arabs warning us hours ahead of enemy attacks from Beersheba. And the opposite was true, there were Arabs informing the Turks of our movements too.

ARAB VILLAGE LIFE

George recalls:

> Each morning the inhabitants of a nearby village streamed out moving up and down the narrow wadi just at the rear of our hangars. They made a picturesque sight as they followed a couple of Arabs in flowing garments seated on camels. The followers wore a variety of similar natural garments as was their custom as they travelled along on camels, horses mules and donkeys.
>
> The older Arabs rode horses and donkeys whereas the remainder including all the women and children travelled on foot carrying primitive agricultural implements to the lower grounds where they tended their crops.
>
> There were about one hundred of them like one large family passing silently by in one direction in the mornings returning each day at about four o' clock in the afternoon. Their donkeys, mules and camels returned loaded with hay and cut vegetation. The men rode and the women walked along carrying bundles of hay and other produce while the children usually carried tools.
>
> It was like a silent ghostly procession each day as they seemed so unconcerned by the thousands of troops then facing Gaza. They simply and silently trudged along with eyes of filled with wonder as they looked at our machines and us as we in our turn stood on the higher ground watching them and their passing.
>
> The sight had made me anxious to see inside that village and so one day with a couple of hours free with another mechanic for company I ventured into a nearby pretty Arab village surrounded by palm trees. There we could witness the Arab way of life at first hand. It was actually the first time during our advance to Gaza that we had ever seen a village except on the occasion when I flew over El Arish, on the coast south of Gaza, with Bannatyne.
>
> As we moved forward we saw two wells within neat walls about two feet high; the whole looking so clean with bare earth trodden and worn over centuries. Further on were ancient flat roofed houses covered with palm leaves with open unglazed windows with shutters ready to close for privacy and protection against sandstorms.
>
> We saw small creatures, lizards and perhaps rats scurrying between the roof covering and top of the stone walls. Coming towards us were four stately

looking young Arabs with ringed head dresses and flowing robes across the shoulders of which were slung the usual bullet loaded bandoliers. Tucked into their belts were revolvers and daggers while rifles were carried over their shoulders.

They walked slowly towards us a suitable distance between each. They looked very dignified with their princely, intelligent sharp well-chiselled features within which were those piercing brown eyes. They looked perturbed at us visitors but we sensed that they could just as suddenly fight without fear if compelled at a second's warning. They came forward as much to say, Are you a friend or enemy?

I just nodded while taking a good look round avoiding any suggestion that we had any ill intentions. Then we retraced our steps back to the camp.

They were the gods and masters of their own people, keen and alert at all times. Clean and honest looking and so different from the assortment of Arabs we had seen in Egypt. More like the Arabians that Lawrence had gathered about him in his campaign. These had a life indifferent to either Turks or British.

Nevertheless the village had been searched because they could have mounted a damaging attack at night on our drome. It would have been so easy for an enemy agent to signal our position to enemy pilots from there which I believe happened on that first night raid.

In later years I often look back in my mind's eye to that village when I read about the Gaza strip which the Arabs had been compelled to leave. Nasir's son told us in 1945, here in Liverpool in the British Council premises that had been a heavy blow to them, losing all that they had fought for. I thought of them compelled now to live in shacks.

A few days later on my way to Arabia as a member of a party with a dispatch to join Lawrence, I was able to relax sitting on some cases in my open truck looking for the last time at the Gaza hills where thousands of men had gathered, many never to return. I realise now how Lawrence's plan to strike through the back door had saved many of those lives.

British forces steadily advanced working up the coast line setting up routes by sea and rail from Katara [Kantara]. Our soldiers foot slogged their way while the Australians with camel transport brought food and ammo as we prepared at Rafa for the Gaza attack. A mile a day the Royal Engineers constructed a railway near the front line patrolled in the rear to prevent enemy attempts to destroy our supply water line. Protection was also provided by patrols of the Scottish Light Horse and the newly organised Australian Camel Corps.

In 1917 Australian and other Allied troops advanced into Palestine and captured Gaza and Jerusalem; by 1918 they had occupied Lebanon and Syria.

NOVEMBER/DECEMBER 1917

GEORGE HAS BAD TOOTH TREATED IN SUEZ

At one time on X Flight's drome, George developed an abscess in his right gums, just after his return from an advanced ground at Decie, and for the first time in his service he had to report for medical attention. The naval doctor from HMS *Humber* arrived at the camp to treat him.

My face was all swollen, and after being examined in a bell tent, the doctor decided that we would have to pull out a back tooth.

I was held up against the tent pole, with my assistant to steady my head, whilst the Doctor was injecting some cocaine into the gums, and then started the operation to extract the tooth. The cocaine mixture consisted of some tablets dissolved in water that seemed to have been in stock for many years. The British Tommy needed good 'biters' to cope with our daily ration of Army 'dog biscuits'.

The MO got his metal tooth extractor on the tooth, twisting and pulling, with the sweat running down our three faces. Toby Wheeler held my head, the doctor pulling like hell and I feeling that he was going to pull half my gums out. The MO gave up. I pulled out my shirt to wipe the sweat off my face. Both Wheeler did the same and the doctor having a nice large handkerchief, wiped his face with it then passed it over to Wheeler and me.

The doctor asked, 'Was the cocaine okay?'

I replied, 'No use at all. You pulled hell out of me, I thought you were trying to pull my head off!'

'I failed,' said he. 'The only time ever! You will have to go to Suez. Fortunately there is a ship arriving this evening and you must go on it. I will send a note with you along with another of your men who has to report to Egypt. You must have that out as soon as possible!'

The next day McCloud and I set off for Suez. When we landed there, I went straight to the Army Dental Hospital, and the operation was done under gas putting me at ease. I then reported to the Suez Drome for overnight accommodation as instructed ready for my return to Aquaba on the next ship sailing from Suez to our base in Arabia.

Except for a couple of occasions we had received no pay in Arabia, ten pounds, leaving about thirty pounds to my credit. The boys had given me a list of their requirements; cigs, tooth paste, soaps, sweets, chocolate and other such items so I went into Suez to do my shopping.

And, finally after drawing another ten quid, I filled about eight sand bags with my shopping and kept them handy till my return having been told that the boat could be about another two weeks. In the mean time I could walk down to Suez at times to enjoy a nice chicken meal, and a nice cool beer on ice.

HANDLEY PAGE BOMBER

According to one source, in August, 1918, one Handley Page biplane O/400 was flown from England out to the Middle East. (George says he saw one there in November 1917.) Later, on 22 November 1918 Major Ross Smith landed a Handley Page near Um-el-Jemal bringing cries from the Arabs of, 'indeed they have sent us "the" aeroplane of which the others are but foals!'[23]

George recounts:

> I remembered the Handley Page bomber that Colonel Barton had chartered to bring fuel and supplies to Azrak to assist Junor and Murphy in attacking their enemies' aircraft nests. That Handley Page was the first of its kind to be flown out to Egypt from England arriving in Suez in November 1917. There I had experienced the pleasure of looking over it and taking part in its refuelling while waiting for a ship to take me back to Aquaba on Christmas Day 1917.
>
> The pilot of that machine on that journey was a Colonel McLaren who had joined the RFC at Gosport as a mechanic but left to be granted a Commission in a Scottish regiment, returning a couple of weeks later in his regimental uniform wearing Scotch plaid trousers.
>
> McLaren came out with us and became a very efficient pilot in operations around Romani before its fall. Our Commanding Officer was then, Lord Leighton, an old fashioned aristocrat who was very conscious of his title and professional importance. He was far too keen on spit and polish, very different from Lords Selby and Lucas who valued comradeship in war.

The edition of *Flight* published on 21 August 1914 shows:

> R.F.C.—Military Wing.—Appointments to take effect from June 30th, 1914: To be Flying Officers ....To the Reserve—Major Sir Bryan B. M. Leighton, Bt., Westmorland and Cumberland Yeomanry and Flight, March 12 1915, Flying Officer: Lieut.-Col. Sir B. B. M. Leighton, Bart., Territorial Force Reserve, from the Reserve. Dated Feb. 5th, 1915.

And yet there is a Captain John Burgh Talbot Leighton who was born on 9 February 1892, the son of Sir Bryan Baldwyn Mawddwy Leighton, 9th Bt, who died on 7 May 1917 at the age of twenty-five, from wounds received in practice. It is written that Captain John Burgh Talbot Leighton fought in the First World War, where he was mentioned in despatches twice. He gained the rank of Captain in the service of the Scots Guards then gained the rank of Squadron Commander in the service of the RFC. He was decorated with the award of Military Cross (MC).

In November 1917, the main No. 14 Squadron operated out of an aerodrome at Wadi Surar, 8 miles west of Jerusalem, re-equipped with RE8 aircraft improvements upon the old BE2c machines. For them operations had moved from the plains of Sinai and the southern Palestine coast to the Judean Hills. Bad weather in Wadi Surar during December 1917 had seriously impeded flying when the ground became waterlogged after heavy rain. Squadron members discovered that by hauling their aeroplanes up the nearest hill and launching downwards they could become airborne. X Flight was one of the detached flights of the squadron.

Wadi Surar is the Arabic name for the place Nahal Sorek where Delilah lived and where she persuaded Samson to tell her the secret of his strength and betrayed him (see Book of Judges, 16:4). Its geographical importance lies in the fact that it is one of the largest, most important drainage basins in the Judean Hills.

The weekly reports of the Flight commanders were written as objectively as possible following an agreed pattern under subheadings such as: 'FLYING; M.T. (Motor Transport); WORKSHOPS; GENERAL.' In fact the accounts of workshop activities are much more revealing of the kinds of work the mechanics like George would be carrying out than were his own writings. Beardmore engines were constantly being stripped down, cleaned and re-assembled; certainly in Akaba, if not in the advanced landing grounds in which George spent much of his time. In those reports the commanders referred to themselves in the third person as in a report written and signed by Furness-Williams in April 1918:

> Some camels and men hidden behind 'EB', number about '50'. Whether hostile or friendly unknown. Capt Furness-Williams, 2/Lts Makins and Junor left to bomb TEL EL SHAHM but Capt. Furness-Williams burst a tyre.

Living conditions at the advanced landing grounds were graphically described in a letter home written by Frank Birkinshaw, one of George's mechanic colleagues:

> The last five days I have been up at the advanced Aerodrome, doing nothing except lying under my mosquito net and dividing my time between swatting flies and wishing I were in the Arctic region. Really it has been very hot just lately, even our drinking water is quite hot and I am sure that anyone who started an ice-cream industry would make his fortune.[24]

Frank Thornton Birkinshaw, born in 1898, ran off to war at the age of sixteen in service with the Royal Warwickshire Regiment. Six months after a posting to France he contracted rheumatic fever and was repatriated to recover from his illness. He then joined the RFC in February 1917 and was sent to Arabia in November of that year. There he remained as a member of X Flight until early 1919. Although styled as a driver he was actually an Air Mechanic, finishing the war as a Corporal. A very able young man, he eventually became a medical doctor.

December 1917

X Flight Report

The X Flight Report for the week ending 9 December 1917 was signed by Lt Siddons in Akaba.

He went out searching for an overdue machine.

At 6.00 am on 7th a search party consisting of Major Lawrence, 2/Lieut. Morgan, Sgt. Rhind and A.M. Forder left AKABA for ELTHEMED. Car broke down 8 miles from AKABA owing to stripped planet wheel differential. Major Lawrence and 2/Lieut. Morgan walked back to AKABA. Several of their aircraft went in search. Lawrence going up with Capt. Croil and landing occasionally to ask natives about the missing aircraft to no avail but in fact the machine had landed safely about 120 miles South of AKABA on the east side of the Gulf.

The X Flight Report for the week ending 23 December 1917 was signed by Lt Siddons in Akaba.

2/Lieut. Nunan flying in from SUEZ was missing. On the 24th it was learned that he had to land about six miles from ELTHEMED. Rations and blankets were sent out to him as spares were expected from SS *Buriana* the next day. Nunan was being looked after by Bedouins.

George flies with the Squadron Commander at the Battle of Jaffa Hill

George recounts:

I recall being selected by my Squadron Commander to play a small part in the Battle of Jaffa, 1917. And the first in the ranks to be given the task as gunner observer to him, Major P. Bannatyne. [Bannatyne became commander of No. 14 Squadron on 1 July 1916.]

He called out, 'Hynes get a petrol funnel, and some tools and put them in my machine, also put some warm underclothing on, and be ready to take off at four thirty.' and then he left me with not one more word of what was to come.

I didn't know until the following morning when we got all our machines in the air at dawn, four fifteen. Ours was the last to leave our advanced landing ground a few miles north of El Arish because it was established practice that the leader always saw his machines off, then following in their wake.

In the Sinai three main routes came together at El Arish close to the border with Palestine. All aircraft operating out of there were obliged to carry four days' rations of food and water, rifle and ammunition, a signal pistol, smoke bombs and strips of cloth to lay out on the ground as signals if forced to land. Airmen often sewed gold coins into their tunics to pay Bedouins for their safe return to British lines.

45

George continues:

I had swung the prop of his engine for a quick engine run up when Bannatyne said 'Go and get your tunic and helmet!' so I ran towards my heap of clothing. I was wearing only my army gym issue pumps on my feet, my shorts and my grey issue shirt. Bannatyne, unaware of what I had in mind when I started at the gallop, shouted for me to halt and compelled me to double back and get into the machine. 'Jump in Hynes, we are due over our naval vessels by half past four.' I jumped into the cockpit and as we were taking the run for take off, I loaded my Lewis gun ready for action and soon we were airborne over the Med following the coastline to take part in the Battle of Jaffa.

We flew over the naval vessels which were covering the Australian troops and the supporting British troops driving the Turks towards their own consolidated positions on Jaffa Hill. At about a height of 2000 feet, we flew over the ships. Bannatyne signalled with his Morse key and turned towards Jaffa Hill in support of Australia No. 1 Squadron and our No. 14 Squadron who were dropping their bomb loads on the enemy redoubts, trenches and retreating troops.

Our machine dropped our half load of bombs, full loads were only carried when there was no observer in these latest improvised BE 2Cs. The first of that type we had ever received and staying with us during the rest of our operations.

The BE2C had a top plane extension of wing area that gave the machine greater lift and greater speed due to being fitted with the more economical 90-horsepower RAF engine. The aircraft was nicknamed Fokker Fodder on the Western Front because it was slow and cumbersome. Throughout X Flight's career the BEs survived because of the loving attention they received from mechanics like George and the ingenious pilots who flew them.

George continues:

The day before I had my initiation in the use of the gun there for the defence of the pilot. When there was no observer, the pilot had to operate the gun with one hand while manipulating the joystick with the other! Sometimes both hands were needed to reload a drum and then it was a case of controlling the machine with knees. In combat, in the air, without a fighter machine escort it was all down to the pilot's skill against an enemy while diving, looping the loop, side slipping; the pilot hoping to be able to catch his attacker at a time when he was most vulnerable.

Our pilots were up to all the tricks. They needed to be in what was really a suicide machine over the lines. I must give great credit to our pilots who were fearless having to battle against an enemy who had the Taube and the Fokker long before ours were issued with the Sopwith Pup and the Bristol in the Sinai campaign, our first advance.

During our flight I stayed alert and ready to cover my pilot keeping a good look out as we flew over Jaffa Hill where all the action was. Major Bannatyne was concentrating on an enemy who was surprised by our attack on previously agreed positions and targets. There were no enemy planes in sight when Bannatyne told me that now was the chance to have a go with our gun. 'Enjoy yourself as I dive over the enemy troops!' I knelt on my observer's seat with the safety catch off and ready for the word go.

My pilot did a starboard side slip, 'Get ready to give them a burst!' as I swung my gun downwards in an area patrolled by a few Australians of the mounted brigade their direction

'Now, it's yours!' and I used my ninety-seven round drum on the trenches as we sailed over the positions at about four hundred feet. My pilot then began his climb towards the sea, turning away and heading for the flat landing ground just at the rear of our attacking troops.

We landed on the first grass-covered flat that we had been on since leaving England. The landing ground was surrounded by high hills protecting the inland flanks of our main advancing troops. Major Bannatyne went back with Dempsey to confirm the report for Cairo while our infantry vanguard were moving forward that same night in the wake of the Australian Light Horse patrols. The advance guards were the Manchesters. I had moved forward with a small party of the mechanics to receive our aircraft which were to follow at dawn the next morning. The Manchesters arrived about five hours after us and settled down with us till dawn.

I felt much warmer then in a very hot sunshine than on that dawn flight with only my shorts, shirt and helmet in the chilly morning atmosphere. We were kept very busy with our machines landing and taking off regularly and the close rattle of rifle and machine gun fire. We had a snack with our two pilots Bannatyne and Freeman.

The Battle of Jaffa Hill was a minor engagement which took place across the two days of 21 and 22 December 1917.

The Australian No. 1 Squadron (formerly No. 67 RFC) gave close support to Lawrence who would sometimes be flown about by Capt. Ross Smith. Lawrence would, of course, sit in the observer's seat. An extract from a letter written by Mr Leslie Hunt and published in *Flight* on 16 December 1960, recounts:

One burly digger pilot told Lawrence, 'You wouldn't make a batman to a padre' and seconds later cried for mercy as he lay writhing after a short bout of wrestling. 'Gee,' he said to his cobbers, 'this pommie has muscles like piano wires!'

Most of X Flight were in Akaba in December 1917. T.D. Siddons was in Command. In December 1917 Brigadier-General A.E. Borton was appointed

Commander of the Palestine Brigade RFC. 'Biffy' Borton has been attributed with invented the slang term 'Archie' for anti-aircraft fire because Borton used to shout, 'Archibald, certainly not', from a popular music-hall song written by George Robey as he flew between the exploding German shells.

X FLIGHT REPORT

The X Flight Report for the week ending 23 December 1917 was signed by Lt Siddons in Akaba.

Among other matters it was reported that 2/Lieut Nunan had failed to arrive from Suez although he had flown out in good time. (S.C. Nunan was a member of the Australian No. 1 Squadron.) He later took part in the machine gunning of retreating Turks on 21 September 1918 as they passed through a gorge on the Wady Fara road. As the attacks continued throughout the day the Turkish survivors waved white flags. But, wrote Conrick, 'it was quite impossible for us to accept the surrender of the enemy, so we just kept on destroying them.' Another No. 1 Squadron observer, L.W. Sutherland, called it 'sheer butchery'.[25]

SHIP EXPLODES

George recalls:

> At last I had orders to pack up and myself and my stock, after arriving at the seafront, were transported by naval pinnace to board a ship anchored in the Bay.
>
> As we were heading across the bay, we heard an Almighty explosion aboard the ship and saw a flash amidships while flames shot upwards. We returned to the wharf where the crew reported back to their Transport Office. We learnt later that the Captain was killed and the ship burnt itself out for a few days. I had to return to Suez camp and the Drome.
>
> It was about a week later when I set off again, on a ship carrying supplies including two Crossley cars which would increase our Flying Attachment to four tenders. It was in one of those tenders that I made my living quarters during my journey back.

In his report for the week ending 30 December 1917 Siddons recorded the arrival of the two Crossleys on SS *Buriana*. The Leyland lorry which also arrived could not be landed on the pier and had to be off-loaded on a sandy beach nearby.

> Strict orders from Naval Transport were that no ship should go through the Suez Canal after coaling or taking on supplies until the Captain was told the day appointed by the Naval Office. Meanwhile the ship must stay in the Bay, and nobody was allowed on or off the ship during its stay there except for officials such as service personnel who would be taken across on craft from the Naval Office. The reason was to prevent attempts by enemies to place

timed explosives during the coaling or in any of the goods placed on board. Ships might lie at anchor for three or four days or more as determined the Naval Office.

Those precautions were designed to prevent ships being sunk and blocking the Canal. Similar precautions were taken along the whole length of the Canal by patrols with horses pulling skids along to smooth over the sand. Footprints in the sand would indicate unauthorised crossings. An intruder would have to be a long distance jumper to cross those sands without detection by our patrols.

CHRISTMAS DAY 1917

Meanwhile George arrived back in the advanced drome.

> I arrived back on Xmas day about eleven in the morning, and some of my comrades had met me with a Crossley, and helped with my sand bags, and in excited welcomes asked, 'Have you seen Furness-Williams [the CO]? He has gone over to Suez to bring us back some beer. He told us that we were going to have some luxury in Aquaba, and celebrate because Xmas comes but once a year!' He has gone by air, and is going to bring it back on a machine.
>
> I asked, 'When did he go?'
>
> 'Yesterday afternoon.'
>
> 'I was then on the ship so I would not have met him.'
>
> I arrived back in my hangar, with the boys looking for their wants, so I opened my sand bags, and dished out according to the list I had made out. Everyone was happy; especially when we saw the machine flying in from Suez about midday.

George continues:

> Captain Furness-Williams had arrived from Suez and was circling the aerodrome with his Xmas load secured under the bomb racks for a landing. He knew that he had to glide in carefully if he was to make a good landing.
>
> I was hoping all would be well as I was more concerned about his safety than the beer in the two wooden crates strapped one on each bomb rack under the port and starboard wings. The flat heads on the crates acted like a first step towards the invention of air brake landing flaps on the aircraft of today.
>
> Williams completed two circuits of the drome and came in over the thick scrub and sand dunes heading for the flat in the direction of the Gulf beach and there made a perfect landing. It was a sigh of relief when our chaps went out to swing his machine around to taxi to our canvas hangars and Williams got out happily smiling.
>
> He spoke, 'Well I have brought you a little to put a nice new taste on your tongues this Xmas Day. There are also some bottles of whisky for the officers. Put them in the tent. Sorry, George, I could not pick you up from

Suez. In any case I was told you were on your way back and all was well!'

At some time after the war, I read that the reporter Lowell Thomas had told everyone that the machine had crashed, the beer had been lost and the mechanics had said, 'We would have rather seen his blood flowing to waste rather than the beer!' or words to that effect.

In his memoirs, George wrote, 'His statement is incorrect!'

One feels sure that it was, but Lowell Thomas with his reporter's feel for a good punch line must have knowingly invented a humorous ending!

George continues:

We had work to carry out on our machines on Christmas Day but Furness-Williams gave orders that we be granted an extra ration of bully beef with two boiled onions, about three pounds of boiled potatoes, extra boiled rice and a bottle of Crown Pilsener beer each. All that together with the cigs that I brought in made it a most enjoyable Christmas Day.

We had every reason to be grateful for that because no other person had done anything towards our care during our 'advance operations'. To many we were just a group obeying orders from Cairo. But we did it well without grumbling helping Lawrence to achieve his plans to beat the Turks.

X FLIGHT REPORT

The X Flight Report for the week ending 30 December 1917 was signed by Lt Siddons in Akaba, saying that on the morning of the 24th a message had been received by camel from Lt Nunan giving his position as 6 miles from Elthemed. A car party had gone out getting within a few miles of Elthemed but there they were told there were no aircraft near there so it returned but blankets and rations were eventually sent to Nunan. Another letter from Nunan said that Bedouins were looking after him.

George continues:

Having been settled into our landing ground by Lieutenant Siddons the enemy positions were surveyed and our machines carried out some bombing raids on Maan and Mudowarrra with the additional pilots, Divers and Makin.

We returned to Aquaba after bombing according to plan helping the Arab sorties in November when I was compelled to go to Suez for treatment. Lieutenants Oldfield and Latham arrived increasing our complement of pilots. When I returned on Christmas Day I was able to pass detailed information about the Beardmore engines and air frames to our own mechanics. None of them had worked on this type of Martinsyde Scout whereas I had been on them in Sinai when the squadron was replacing and BE2Cs. They then got busy checking them all over.

The usual early dawn reconnaissance and bombing went on but a little more time could be spent as more hands gained experience in servicing. By then, October, I had been promoted to corporal gaining more freedom to get down to it and to help the chaps adjust to our conditions.

Furness-Williams, who had a lovely, enthusiastic personality kept on trying to give us some recreation as an alternative to our constant work load.

BOXING DAY 1917

George continues:

> Furness-Williams together with Joyce and the commander of HMS *Humber*, arranged a sports meeting on our drome for the benefit of the boys and to entertain Emir Feisal on Boxing Day. [That would have been Wednesday 26 December 1917.] During the early morning our machines flew over Maan with a repeat raid in afternoon to let the enemy know we were not sleeping. We kept the Turks guessing.
>
> An Egyptian band comprising twelve musicians provided background music. Races were arranged along with a game of football which the Arabs joined in. There were camel races, horse races and also a long distance run by one of our mechanics named Howard who was an experienced runner back in England.
>
> A row of army benches was set out for Feisal, the guest of honour, and his staff and bodyguards in attendance. Our officers had clubbed together to provide the equivalent of ten one pound notes in Egyptian money.

Emir Feisal, born in 1885, was the third son of Sherif Ibn Hussein, King of the Hejaz. He believed that he was descended directly from the Prophet Mohammed. Lawrence chose him as the most impressive of the princes as a partner in his plans to defeat the Turks. His 'army' was made up of Arab irregulars, Turkish prisoners and deserters. Lawrence described him as '…very tall and pillar-like, very slender, in his long white silk robes and his brown headcloth bound with brilliant scarlet and gold cord.' After the war he failed to gain Arab self rule from the Council of Ten, the English, French and American governments, and after an attempt at rebellion reluctantly accepted the kingship of Iraq.

George continues:

> Between our duties on aircraft maintenance, we took our turns in the races after inviting the Arabs to join in. Mostly, they enjoyed kicking the ball in their bare feet. That must have been tough as they slammed the ball.
>
> For a bit of fun, for further entertainment, our boys borrowed the band instruments and as I had already learned to play the cornet gave them tunes from memory, a very popular selection called 'Nursery Rhymes'. The other lads just blew anything simply to kick up a row. Wheeler played the bass drum, as was just the chap to come up with some funny antics.

The 'foo foo' band prompted the Egyptians and Arabs to join in by hand clapping to our horrible melodies. They really enjoyed the tom-foolery. The event ended with the winners of each race being awarded their prizes by Emir Feisal, our officers all sitting alongside him. Furness-Williams advised Feisal how many notes were to be presented to each winner.

When receiving their winnings, our chaps saluted the officers and bowed to Feisal. This whole stunt had shown that Britishers could be amusing friends as well as battle partners. We had no refreshments for our guests but that was not expected in these circumstances and everything went off well. Lawrence was away between Aquaba and Cairo.

JANUARY 1918

X FLIGHT REPORT

The X Flight Report for the week ending 5 January 1918 was signed by Lt Siddons in Akaba.

> A salvage party went out to repair Nunan's machine. 2/Lieuts Murphy and McGuinness arrived by air on 2 Jan. and on 4th Siddons and Murphy were bombing MAAN and AIN OHEIDA.' [Murphy and McGuinness were from the Australian squadron.)
>
> 2/Lieut. Nunan flew in from ELTHEMED after having the leading edge of one plane mended with a wing skid and all the pistons lapped in valves ground in and small ends bushes refitted. But owing to the non-arrival of sufficient Beardmore spares Nunan's machine was unserviceable from its arrival.

Here it is mentioned that a wire had gone to Perardua, presumably RFC HQ. *Per ardua* is of course the first two words of the subsequent RAF motto, *Per Ardua ad Astra*.

Under the subheading 'Workshops' there is an interesting entry typical of the entries made in the weekly reports. It is indicative of the ingenuity exercised 'in the field'.

> A pulley of aluminium and duralumin was cast turned and fitted to a magneto for running a plug tester driven from the Workshops grindstone. Difficulty was experienced in making the plug tested proof against 90 lbs pressure. Electric light was fitted to the 3 hangars on the east side of Aerodrome and to the engine repair Shops.

As the distilling plant had not arrived one was made from petrol tins and copper tubing distilling sufficient water for the Martinsydes.

George recalls:

During the those operations Furness-Williams had consolidated more action from Decie, and kept about four to five machines and their pilots in camp with us and the remainder operating from our base in the Wadi Araba. During those dawn until dusk operations our flying time had been decreased by two thirds because the enemy's two strongholds were then only ten minutes' flying time away at Mudowwara. Maan was twenty minutes away as it was about the same distance from Mudowwara to Maan as Aquaba was to Maan.

During these operations Furness-Williams was in command at Decie and Lieutenant Siddons in command at Aquaba, both using a similar number of aircraft. Lawrence, the Arabs and armoured cars had made a very heavy attack on Mudowwara supported by our machines during the latter end of or stay at Decie. Four Martinsydes had joined us.

X FLIGHT REPORT

The X Flight Report for the week ending 12 January 1918 was signed by Lt Siddons in Akaba.

It was a substantial document filled with operational details. The Flight attacked many places during its operative life and flew many more reconnaissance flights during that time. For example, during the first couple of months of 1918 places where X Flight dropped bombs included the following: at least ten times on Mudhawara, twenty times on Ma'an, then Akabat el Hejazia station and several times each on places such as Aneiza, Bir Basta Jurf el Dervish, Nagb el Eshtar – Ma'an road, Semna, Wadi Retham, Wadi el Jourdun and several trains here and there.

The territory around Ma'an was an eerie deserted moonscape of chasms and gorges ranging between 1,000 to 4,000 feet deep, composed of granite, basalt and porphyry. The flat areas were filled with jagged volcanic rock fragments and sometimes covered in soft dark sand and weathered sandstone. To say the least it was a pitiless, unforgiving region.

The planes flew reconnaissance over additional places: Abu Jerdun, Abu le Sal, Abu Lisal, Abu Lawana, Abu Lesan, Abu Suwana, Ain Sadeika, Ain Uheida, Akabat el Hejazia, Aneiza, Batia, Bir el Shedia, Dajaniya, Decie, Fasoa, Ghadir el Haj, Jurf el Deruish, Kalaat, Kerikia,'M Reiga, Ramleh, Semana, Shedia, Tel el Shahm, Wadi Retham and Wadi Jourdon. Sometimes several times each.

X FLIGHT REPORT

The X Flight Report for the week ending 19 January 1918 was signed by Lt Siddons in Akaba 'for' Capt. Commanding X Flight, RFC.

On the 19th, Capt. Furness-Williams with 2 cars, 7 other ranks and considerable stores and 10 days rations left AKABA for SAWANA where a forward landing ground had been chosen for operations against the line.

53

The report continues:

> On the 17th Capt. Furness-Williams arrived and took over command.
> On the 17th, 2Lieut. Makins returned from EL GUEIRA having found a landing ground at ABU SAWANA… Personnel travelled by car to set up an advanced ground at SAWANA.

There must have been a constant stream of ship arrivals in the port of Akaba because in this one report alone three are mentioned, SS *Arethusa*, SS *Burriana* and HMS *Hardinge*.

One inscription records a visit by HMS *Hardinge*, the ship which hovered so effectively along the Arabian shore during the Arab Revolt and which the Arabs thought must be peaceably inclined because she had only one funnel.[26]

In a letter home, dated 1 January 1918, Air Mechanic Birkinshaw, of X Flight, tellingly and colourfully described his first camel ride.

> If you received my last letter you will remember I told you that I was going on a little trip, partially by camel. I left the same day and had a ripping time. There was only myself and an officer, together with six or seven camel men, and as I had never ridden a camel before I had a most agonizing time the first two days. You see camels get up in three motions like a switchback and when they eventually get right up, one seems miles away from the ground. After the first day's ride I felt like a heap of cinders that has just been shaken through a sieve, but I soon got used to it and now I am quite an expert camel rider. We slept in all sorts of weird places, amongst them being a castle built by the Emperor Saladin, an old Turkish fort, a cave in the rocks, a ditch and a dry river bed, and we actually saw streams and green grass, both of course being absolutely foreign to the country around here.[27]

The X Flight Report for the week ending 26 January 1918 was signed by Capt. Furness-Williams in Akaba.

Capt. Furness-Williams was signing as Capt. RFC, Commanding X Flight, Royal Flying Corps. SS *Race Fisher* is mentioned and attacks on Mudhawara.

X FLIGHT REPORT

In a special X Flight Report for the week ending 28 January 1918 Furness-Williams reported RFC co-operation with Arabian and other troops in an attack on Mudhawara station on the Hejaz railway.

Between 10 January and 4 February 1918, the Battle of Tafileh took place between a Turkish regiment, commanded by Lieutenant-Colonel Hamid Fakhri Bey, acting GOC 48th Division and the Allied troops. Fighting on the Turkish side were the 3/151 Regiment, 1/152 Regiment, a murettab (a composite, of various units) battalion of 150, a company of gendarmes, a detachment of 100 cavalry, two Austrian quick-firing mountain guns, and twenty-three machine guns. The Turks were beaten at Tafileh and Fakhri Bey was killed.

Lawrence took part in the battle for Tafilah (Tafileh), then returned to Feisal's base at Gueira for funds and advice. Today, Tafilah is a small city with a population of 35,000 people in south Jordan 180 km from Amman. It is famous for its green gardens filled with olive and fig trees and grape vines because it is well watered by many natural springs.

FEBRUARY 1918

X FLIGHT REPORT

The X Flight Report for the week ending 2 February 1918 was signed by Capt. Furness-Williams in Akaba.

Information was given about the use of wireless sets for co-operation with the Navy and the Bombing of Ma'an. Also, a decision had to be made about using Decie and/or Gueira as landing grounds.

In this report, under the heading FLYING, he wrote:

> On the 27th 1-100 lbs quarter second delay action bomb was tested and on 29th 25 sec delay fuses of our own design for 100 lbs were tested in the sea, the latter without success. On 30th 2/Lt. Nunan, tested another 25 sec. Delay action bomb in the Wadi ARABA but the primer exploded without detonating the whole bomb. The experiments are proceeding.

He also mentioned a car breakdown in January at Decie and a crashed Martinsyde at Abu Suwana.

In the *Seven Pillars of Wisdom*, Book 6, Lawrence mentioned staying in Abu Sawana in November 1917 saying there was a water pool there. It would have therefore been an ideal place for an advanced drome.

JANUARY TO FEBRUARY 1918

George recalled a football match on the drome.

> A few days after our sports day, a Turkish aircraft had been shot down at Gueira by Arab rifle fire. The pilot had been taken over by our Flight Commander who took him into his tent till a ship arrived to take him to Cairo. The Arabs had destroyed his machine and stripped it and him of all his clothing. He was lucky to have escaped alive but he had not been injured. It turned out that the Turk, about 26 years of age, had been a school teacher and was good at football.

Here was one of those instances when an enemy 'knight of the air' was rescued and treated in accordance with a code of chivalry not unlike the ways of the medieval knight.

Furness-Williams arranged a football match on our landing ground and the pilot played on one of the sides. We managed to get a full twenty-two players. Williams enjoyed himself shouting, 'Go the Reds!' One chap from London who was a good player made it his business to give the Turk a few tough shoulder charges but we appealed to him to go steady.

A rumour went about that an attempt was to be made to rescue him but Furness-Williams mounted guards on the marquee at night until finally the prisoner was put on the ship for Egypt. However, that same afternoon a couple of our boys had gone up to bring the Benz engine from the fire wreckage. They discovered some packets of steel darts which the Germans had put into action on the Western Front to drop on our troops. When the British and French responded with the same kind of weapon the Germans started to squeal. When we hit back like that the Germans stopped using them so we stopped too.

Furness-Williams became very angry on seeing those steel darts, 'If I had known that that bastard had those to drop on our Arabs, I would have kicked his arse! We would not have treated him like a guest.'

Were they unaware that a report published in *Flight* on 4 January 1917 mentions shortages of RFC weapons including 'darts'? The British were at it too.

FURNESS-WILLIAMS TAKES COMMAND OF X FLIGHT

The incident described by George occurred shortly after Furness-Williams had been appointed X Flight's commanding officer in early 1918. *Flight* magazine gives clues to his background with an entry on 15 October 1915, 'The following Aviators' Certificates have been granted: No. 1821 – 2nd Lieut. Frank Harold Furness-Williams, R.F.A. (Maurice Farman Biplane, Military School, Birmingham).' Another entry in *Flight* dated 6 January 1916 records his commission thus 'Temporary 2 Lt. F.H. Furness-Williams, R.A. transferred to general list.'

Another source listing 'RFC and RAF Officers believed to have served in Warwickshire in WW1 and 1920s' has this entry: '25/08/1915 15/01/1916 2/Lt Frank Harold Furness-Williams 5 Reserve Aeroplane Squadron, 19 Squadron.'[28]

For his otherwise unrecognised work with X Flight he was awarded the Order of Al Nahda, listed as serving with No. 14 Squadron RFC.[29]

According to *Winged Promises*, a history of No. 14 Squadron, in January 1918 Captain F. H. Furness-Williams took command of X Flight. George probably meant that F.W. had arrived in No. 14 Squadron in October 1917.

X FLIGHT REPORT

The X Flight Report for the week ending 17 February 1918 was signed by Capt. Furness-Williams in Akaba.

On Thursday 14th 2/Lt. Makins and driver went to EL GUEIRA to see if they could find the Turkish pilot who had a forced landing E. of KALAAT ANEIZA and had been captured by Arabs. He eventually found that the prisoner had been sent to AKABA and traced him to the prisoners' camp. All his clothes had been taken away and he had been very badly treated. I obtained authority to get him away from the Turkish prisoners' camp and for the moment he is living with us before proceeding by ship to Egypt. I have interrogated him and the information is attached.

The information received from 2/Lieut Ismail Zaki, a captured Turkish pilot, is given here.

He is 19 years of age and learnt to fly at St. Stefano (preliminary instruction) in 1915 and then went to Berlin for further instruction. The instructors and system there was good and the pilots turned out were good. His course there lasted 7 months. They have 3 machines at Maan, all Rumplers, and there is an Albatross B.U. Scout and Halberstadts coming to make a total of 5 or 6 machines.

Their workshops are in good condition.

The effect of our 20 lbs. bombs have been very little but the 100 lbs. bombs very good. One 100 lbs. dropping near engine sheds killed 16 soldiers.

The machines at Maan are not in the sheds but under the ground.

There is an Austrian Sergeant-pilot named Sergt. Sousin, coming to Maan. He is supposed to be a 'crack' pilot and will pilot the Albatross Scout.

He thinks our machines are very good and imagined them to be Bristol Fighters and has always run away from them.

He has been at Maan for 7 months and did 84 hours flying there.

There is a squadron of 7 machines at Amman – 2 Albatross Scouts, 2 Halberstadts, 2 two-seater A.E.G. and 1 Fokker. All the pilots are German except the Fokker pilot.

There are about 2000 rifles, 6 field guns and 250–300 cavalry at Maan, This pilot was shot down by the Arabs at Kalaat Aneiza (North of Maan) and the Arabs cut the wings off the machine. I have traced where his engine (150 H.P. Mercedes) is and am now endeavouring to salve same.

He could give me no information about arrival and departure of trains from Maan.

Signed at AKABA. 21-2-18 by F.H. Furness-Williams Capt. R.F.C., Commanding 'X' Flight, Royal Flying Corps

X FLIGHT'S AIRCRAFT

George wrote that about this time the Flight had received a BE2e, an improved version of the old BE2c. He never entered into any detailed descriptions of the aircraft, probably because he took them and their mechanical characteristics so much for granted in knowing every strut, bolt and pedal. The earliest type of these aircraft were the BE2a and b aircrafts, which were replaced during 1915 by the BE2c, extensively modified by Edward Teshmaker Busk in the hope of gaining more stability. In 1916, the c was replaced by the final version, the BE2e, nicknamed the Quirk.

According to George, X Flight did get at least one BE12, with a more powerful twelve-cylinder RAF engine producing increased speed but it had no observer's seat. It did have a synchronised gun, which fired between the prop blades. He said it was that machine which Captain Junor lost when enemy aircraft at Derra outnumbered him. The BE12 was really more suited to long-range reconnaissance aircraft than aerial combat. Nevertheless Captain G.W. Murlis-Green of No. 17 Squadron shot down several enemy aircraft when flying a BE12.

George recalls:

> Our Flight had increased by six extra machines to a total of ten. We had six pilots who were able to fly any of the three types. The only one lost in action was the previously mentioned BE12. After the campaign, while in Suez, Colonel Grant Dalton told me that was a wonderful record especially with our Martinsydes. He then offered me a position in Egypt.

X FLIGHT REPORT

The X Flight Report for the week ending 25 February 1918 was signed by Capt. Furness-Williams in Akaba.

On the 21st two BE2es arrived to take Lieut. Kirkbride (Intelligence Officer) to Suez.

> 3 cars with bombs and petrol left AKABA for the advanced ground at DECIE on Thursday 21st and arrived back on the 22nd. A mention of changing front wing bars on a Martinsyde and stores arriving from SS BUROLOS.

The arrival of two American filmmakers was not recorded in the February reports or for that matter in any other of the Flight's formal reports of the year. Fortunately George tells us.

AMERICAN FILM MAKERS ARRIVE

George recounts:

> Lawrence, having arrived on Christmas Day, had gone off to join the Arabs and Allenby as they were all on the move. [In a letter dated 14 February 1917 from the Residency in Cairo Lawrence mentions his going to Akaba in two days' time.] Then during our few weeks, preparing for further action, in early January and at short notice, we had neutral visitors in Aquaba. Lowell Thomas and Chase presented themselves at our drome where they were

received by Furness-Williams at a time when most of the camp was resting during the heat of the day. I was introduced to them.

George challenged passages in Richard Adlington's book *Lawrence of Arabia: A Biographical Enquiry*:

> Aldington did assert that Lowell Thomas had portrayed Lawrence in his book, without having proof and evidence of T.E.'s achievements in Arabia and says that he had been invited by Lawrence. He also expressed doubts of when Thomas and Chase landed in Aquaba in 1918. I do know that in Aquaba, in the early part of February, I was introduced to them on our drome on Wadi Araba.

The Wadi is a range of jagged peaks stretching down from the Sea of Galilee, rising steeply from the Jordan Valley, the Dead Sea, at heights of between 4,000 and 6,000 feet. Eastwards stretch plains of flint and gravel and pasture.

Flying in the area was always somewhat daunting as witnessed in a story related in *Flight* about a post-war incident when three Ninaks were flying over some very challenging country between Amman and Akaba. One of the three pilots was a young flying officer within whose aircraft sat a passenger, a government official. When over some perilous country the passenger asked, 'What happens if the engine cuts out?'

The pilot replied, 'Wooden boxes for two!'

The passenger biblically remarked, 'Friend, go up higher!'[30]

Lowell Thomas was an American roving newscaster, film maker and radio presenter throughout the 1920s, and 1930s. Along with his talented cameraman, Harry Chase, he shot moving and still pictures of Lawrence with the Arabs. His film and stories about the '...mysterious blue eyed Arab in the garb of a prince wandering the streets' were very popular. The film was shown to packed audiences in New York and London and in fact in the major cities of the world. There was even a Royal Command Performance.

There is a telling comment in Robert Graves' book *Lawrence and the Arabs*:

> Mr. Lowell Thomas, who has written an inaccurate and sentimental account of Lawrence, links him up with the Northern Irish family of that name and with the famous Indian Mutiny hero 'who tried to do his duty': this is an invention and not a good one.[31]

FEBRUARY 1918 IN WADI ARABA

In his memoirs, George recalled the arrival of Lowell Thomas.

> That [the arrival] occurred about the end of February or the beginning of March, for I remember it clearly, as I had been promoted to the rank of sergeant commencing in March, and just before the formation of the R.A.F. [The Royal Air Force was formed on 1 April 1918.]

Elsewhere in his memoirs, George challenged many passages in Richard Adlington's work, where Aldington expressed doubts about the arrival of Thomas and Chase in Akaba in 1918.[32]

Here George wrote:

> I do know that in Aquaba, in the early part of February, I was introduced to them on our drome on Wadi Araba about a quarter of a mile from Feisal's camp. I know that he had shots of Aquaba, the Gulf and he probably went for car shots up the Wadi Ithm.

Wadi Ithm, is a great chasm of granite opening to the north-cast of the port, a key route to Akaba. It was a direct route to the station of Ma'an on the Hejaz railway but it was so narrow and boulder-blocked that even Lawrence after travelling for several miles up the gorge once turned back.

George continues:

> Lowell Thomas had been in contact with our operations since February. He went on to Gueira, following Feisal's staff, as he could not be with Lawrence or Nasir or on Ali's heels at all times. No cameraman could have undergone such conditions. Information could be gained from our officers in the field, Joyce, Marshall, Hornby and from Feisal, and much information Aquaba [Akaba], and I and others. Our flight was too busy to think of using cine cameras and furthermore, strict military orders forbade carrying them whilst on active service. Although one or two did possess them.

Records of Joyce's service in Hedjaz (Hejaz), 1916–1919, principally official correspondence relating to operations against the Turks in Hedjaz, 1916–1918, and supplies and stores for bases at Rabegh, Wedj [Wejh], Yenbo, Akaba and Abu Lissal, are to be found in the Liddell Hart Centre for Military Archives in King's College, London.

George continues:

> I had a few photos given to me that were taken when I was in advanced positions of one particular busy time in June, and I had one enlarged of Furness-Williams returning from a bomb raid on Mudowwara, and our dog Spot who had spent a few days with us but most times with the armoured cars. He had poked his head in the corner of the picture looking up at the Martinsyde Scout as it was gliding in; that same picture was loaned to the Manager of the Tatler [Cinema] in June 1935, when the Lowell Thomas film was loaned by the British Museum and had been presented by Thomas. I was standing near my machine, a B.E. 2c, that had to be air tested after a partial overhaul, when Williams introduced me, his NCO in charge of the machines. Thomas and Chase appeared to be rather nervous or a little bewildered being in such far different surroundings from those in Palestine but they had a chat with us about our duties in support of Lawrence and the Arabs.

George described the visitors.

> Both wore drill uniforms with pith helmets and they carried their cine camera with a tripod, as they approached me to be introduced by Captain Furness-Williams who had received the two Americans in his marquee when they arrived at our drome in the Wadi Araba.

The 'drome' George refers to was a mere canvas camp set up on some flat desert ground at Wadi Araba. It consisted of a canvas hangar and a few bell tents. Water and food had to be brought in on horses or camels or occasionally by truck, RFC Crossley tenders fitted with double wheels to cope with the rough desert terrain. During the day the temperatures were killingly hot, so hot that pilots and aircraft developed the habit of getting into the air just after dawn at about four thirty in the morning when it was cooler and the air was denser. During the hottest times of the day the air density was so low that it was positively dangerous for aircraft especially when trying to fly over hills.

The Wadi Araba valley is a desert area north of Aquaba City. An arid area, it lies between red sandstone cliffs and narrow gorges for the most part accessible only on foot through sparse scrubland. Today, the valley, 100 miles long and 25 miles wide, is home to a few thousand Bedouin.

Today the Wadi Araba Border Crossing, opened on 8 August 1994, is an international border crossing between Akaba, Jordan and Israel. It is a popular portal used by tourists. This modern political border between Israel and Jordan runs between the Dead Sea and the Gulf of Akaba, separating the Negev from southern Jordan.

George continues:

> After a few minutes talk about our work in support of Lawrence's operations Thomas had asked for an opportunity to take some dramatic shots and consequently, Furness-Williams had decided to give them a picture of our normal every day aircraft operations from our base. I examined the machine and engine tested it and Williams stepped aboard for a take-off.
>
> He got into the cockpit, one of them climbed in the observer's seat. I swung the engine. Then following a thumbs up, the OK sign, from Williams, he made a speedy take-off.
>
> The tripod had been set up at an angle, on the port side to the rear of the BE for best filming and camera shots while airborne. Williams then did a few circuits of the area followed by a short flight towards the Wadi Ithm and the drome returning to report the machine's 'test flight'.
>
> Williams then invited Lowell Thomas to have a trip round over the Gulf and up the Wadi. After a chat with the film operators, he took them up on another flight with Lowell Thomas in the observer's seat. That flight took them over the Gulf, Aquaba [Akaba], the SS *Humber*, the monitor ship, returning to the drome.

After landing, the three then entered Furness-Williams's tent and finally Lowell Thomas and Chase returned to the Aquaba village, most probably in our two Crossley tenders as they could never have trudged over the rough untidy scrub-covered ground with their equipment. I had not seen their departure as I had to go back to my duties on our machines to prepare them for operational duties. I expected they would have been put up on the *Humber*. That was the first and only time I saw Thomas and Chase.

In criticising Adlington, George held that:

Lawrence was not at Aquaba at that time so I can verify that Adlington was incorrect when he stated that Thomas first met Lawrence in Jerusalem in March 1918 when he was a guest at the Duke of Connaught's luncheon.

According to George, to get out to Arabia:

Thomas had had to travel by rail and ship to the Red Sea Naval Transport Office at Port Sudan, then board a ship that would then arrive with supplies at our jetty at Aquaba. Thomas and Chase could not have arrived before May to June.

A fact that supports Lawrence's statement that he only met Thomas during his three-day stay at Aquaba. He returned to his fighting army in early February making contact with Allenby later in March, about the first week. It was then that Lawrence and Allenby were planning the advance. Those are the facts proving that Lawrence had given a true account of his statements in the *Seven Pillars of Wisdom* while Adlington has compiled his statements from his imagination. In fact, in calling Lawrence a charlatan and liar, to his discredit, Adlington was, two months out on that one. It was about four weeks after Lowell Thomas's arrival at Aquaba. When returning from a memorable meeting with Allenby, Lawrence was being flown in an aircraft piloted by Colonel Borton, second in command to General Geoffrey Salmond, Chief Commander of the Middle East RFC. *En route* they had made a forced landing on a sandy plateau off Sinai and I had to be flown out to the downed machine to get them off safely to Aquaba. [According to records, Colonel Borton had arrived in the Middle East on 21 November 1917.]

When criticising certain of Aldington's assertions, George said that Lowell Thomas would never have been able to film any of the ground war simply because it would have been impossible for him and his assistant to carry the cine equipment on the tossing back of a camel going into action! The Decie mudflats where the advanced drome was at the time were never shown in the film; the only shots of aircraft were the ones made in January. George insists that one must realise that Lawrence could not spend time hamming it up for cameramen as he was far too busy fighting a war.

February/ March 1918

X Flight Report

The X Flight, Royal Flying Corps: Summary of Operations for the week ending 2 March 1918 was actually signed by Furness-Williams on 4 March in Ma'an. It reported:

> On the 25th February a reconnaissance of and bomb raid on MA'AN were carried out by two machines. One machine was shot through the oil tank by machine-gun fire and was forced to return but the other continued to WADI EL JORDOUN Station to carry out a reconnaissance. Owing to the fact that this Station is not marked on the map and thought to be ANEIZA.

> On the 28th two machines attempted to do a reconnaissance of ABU SAWANA and MUDHAWARA but were forced to descend owing to engine trouble. On 1st March two machines started out to reconnoitre ABU SUWANA and MUDHAWARA but one returned, being unable to climb.

That fact illustrates the difficulties experienced when the air was too hot and 'thin' to gain height. Furness-Williams went by car to El Gueira advanced ground. Although the report was headed 'ROYAL FLYING CORPS' mention is made of two RAF hangars.

Furness-Williams also wrote:

> On 28th 2/Lt. A.D. Makins and 1/AM Birkenshaw F.J. returned from their search for aeroplane of Turkish pilot who had been brought down by Arab fire. Copy of 2/Lt. Makin's report is enclosed in Qwar Diary for February. The Turkish pilot proceeded to EGYPT by sea on 28th.

X Flight Report

The X Flight Report for the week ending 10 March 1928 was signed by Siddons in Akaba.

> Two B.E. 2es, now on Flight's strength, flown in from SUEZ. Advanced landing grounds in GUEIRA AND DECIE were in use.

X Flight Report

The X Flight, Royal Flying Corps: Summary of Operations for the week ending 16 March 1918 was signed by Furness-Williams in Akaba.

> On the 16th at the request of O.C. Troops AKABA B.E. 2E. B.3681 flew up-country and a message from Major Lawrence was dropped on Arab troops.

George argues:

> Thomas had arrived early in January and my correct story of his arrival is proof that Adlington was very much incorrect in his survey and report that it was about three months later in about April.
>
> It also proves that Lawrence had never met Lowell Thomas before his arrival in January, just before we made another advanced stunt to Decie mudflat. We had been kept very busy co-operating with Lawrence and the Arabs as they advanced into enemy occupied territory taking part in the Battle of Tafilla [Tafileh]. We bombed Maan and Mudowwara repeatedly along with other posts further North keeping the Turks well bedded inside those two strongholds.

George attempted to train as a pilot.

> I had been promoted to sergeant in March 1918 and turned down twice for flying training after being told by General Salmond that I was far too valuable in ground support and pilots' lives were short.

Air Chief Marshal Sir William Geoffrey Hanson Salmond KCB, KCMG, DSO, born in 1878 and most often known as Sir Geoffrey Salmond, was a senior commander in the Royal Flying Corps.

NEWSPAPER INTERVIEW

An article appearing in the *Liverpool Echo and Evening Post* on 28 February 1963 had this to say:

> At that time, young Hynes had never heard of Lawrence. Their first encounter came when orders were received by 14 Squadron to select a team of four planes, four pilots and six expert mechanics, Hynes among them, to form what was known as 'X Flight' for special duties in the Arabian Desert.

George is quoted in the article.

> A party of high ranking Arabs, and a young Army Lieutenant who, let me be frank, looked about the biggest muggins I'd seen in officer's uniform, came along to the briefing. The lieutenant was Lawrence and from then on, our X Flight operated under his orders. I've said he looked a muggins. That's because there was nothing of the ordinary Army officer about him. He was shy, diffident, but when we got to know him, we soon recognised that he was a man you could trust with your life no matter what the odds.[33]
>
> I met Lawrence a dozen times, before the liberation of Damascus and the final capitulation of the Turks brought X Flight's activities to a close and we came home. He was always a friendly easy to talk to man who hated ceremony.[34]

George tells another story featuring Lawrence temporarily stranded in the desert.

It was about four weeks after Lowell Thomas's arrival at Aquaba that Lawrence himself arrived in an aircraft piloted by Colonel Borton, second in command to General Geoffrey Salmond, Chief Commander of the Middle East RFC. I had to go by air [to see] them off safely to Aquaba from a sandy plateau off Sinai where Borton had made a forced landing.

MARCH OR APRIL 1918

GEORGE 'RESCUES' LAWRENCE AND BORTON

George recalls:

I was told by Captain Furness-Williams, my commanding officer, that the pilot of the visiting aircraft had reported Lawrence stranded on Sinai. His machine had made a forced landing because of engine trouble and I had to go out in the visiting aircraft and get him safely to Aquaba. I took tools, funnel and four gallons of aviation spirit.

Our aircraft put down on a sandy plateau and there was Lawrence. He was standing with his pilot near the stranded machine at the only time I ever saw him in a British khaki uniform. Lawrence gave us his unperturbed smile although I thought he looked very comical in that oversized uniform with no belt, wearing a flattened cap looking like a shop dummy wearing an off-the-peg uniform. He wore that uniform for no longer than about ten hours before discarding it in favour of a white cloak from Feisal, and as we heard, equivalent to a status of a Prince of Mecca.

I put the defect right, tested the engine, put it into trim and passed it OK. The take-off was proving to be a very difficult task owing to the very soft sandy conditions and a limited area for the run up. Borton made three cautious attempts but had to pull up each time just short of a sump hole because falling into that would have been disastrous. He would have crashed with T. E. sitting just behind the engine.

I realised that T. E. must be got back safely because the Arabs would never have succeeded without him. Only Lawrence was able to bond them together in a common cause.

I stopped all further attempts until I toured the area and had selected a fresh run fit for take-off. I then advised my pilot to hang on to the wings, I on the port, he on the starboard wing. Borton was advised to rev up the engine to full throttle while we pushed on the machine until I gave the word. Also Borton decided to use a little rudder to allow for the propeller torque to keep the machine on a straight course and to prevent a loss of speed during take-off. That time Colonel Borton managed the take-off [and] much to my relief the machine became air borne. All good pilots knew the importance keeping a straight course and he got her off OK.

Captain Amyas Eden Borton, an officer of the Black Watch (Royal Highlanders) was attached to the RFC. When he and his observer, Captain Anthony Marshall, of the 28th Light Cavalry, Indian Army, also attached to the RFC, were flying a reconnaissance mission over the neighbourhood of Staden, Belgium, on 7 June 1915, Borton was wounded in the head and neck by a bullet fired from a hostile aeroplane.

> …Although suffering severely from loss of blood he continued, with the assistance of the Observer, Captain Marshall, to bandage his wounds and completed the reconnaissance on the prescribed course. His injuries are such that he is not yet out of danger. Captain Marshall continued his observations after rendering all possible aid to the Pilot, who was gradually losing consciousness, notwithstanding that the German aeroplane was persistently attacking.[35]

He was awarded the Distinguished Service Order. He eventually became an Air Vice Marshal having also been awarded Companion of the Order of the Bath, Companion of the order of St Michael and St George, the Air Force Cross and a Mention in Despatches.

George continues:

> The next day T.E. wandered over to our camp on his camel Ghazala alone in the early morning but dressed in an all white Arab dress. He had discarded that khaki uniform he had accepted from Allenby. He thanked me for services rendered on Sinai and continued in the direction of the Gulf.
>
> That is one true story that gives an example why such as men Lord Winterton, Lord Lloyd, Colonel Dawney, Colonel Newcombe, Hornby, Marshall, Buxton and all who took part in the desert operations had a great respect for Lawrence the amateur soldier.

LAWRENCE SMOOTHES SOME RUFFLED ARABIAN FEATHERS

George recounts:

> There is another story that Corporal Wheeler told me. When they were near the end of a journey, the sheik or one of the two sheiks who Lawrence had enticed over from the Turks in that area had jumped up on the rear step of the Crossley that Wheeler and Lat Sefi was travelling in and Sefi kicked the old sheik out of the car!
>
> The sheik picked himself up in a very angry mood and threatened to prevent their entry into his territory. Lawrence came to the rescue and saved a situation that could have brought about the end of Allenby and Lawrence's

plans and would have undone all that Lawrence had achieved. The pilot mentioned had freshly arrived and like Aldington, Bremon and others had a common disdain for those he believed to be among the lower illiterate classes. How could anyone expect to win battles treating the Arabs with dictatorial contempt like that?

I first became aware of that proud, dignified upright bearing of the Arabs in a village set in beautiful Kannunas near the shore of the Med. The place, completely sheltered by palm trees had two wells. The Turks had poisoned one well but left the other untouched allowing the Arab inhabitants to be supplied.

MARCH 1918

X FLIGHT REPORT

X FLIGHT REPORTS during that month mention a raid on MA'AN in which one machine was shot through the oil tank by machine-gun fire and forced to return and that on the 28th of the month, 2/Lt. A.D. Makins and 1/AM Birkinshaw, F.J., returned from a search for the aeroplane of a downed Turkish pilot.

In that report he mentioned heavy rain, a rare commodity indeed during X Flight operations!

APRIL 1918

On 1 April 1918 the Royal Flying Corps became the Royal Air Force.

X FLIGHT REPORT

The second weekly report of X Flight, as an arm of the newly formed Royal Air Force, was written by Captain Furness-Williams, Flight Commander. Here it is given verbatim as a comprehensive illustration of the routine activities of this secret group in its advanced landing grounds.

'X' FLIGHT ROYAL AIR FORCE

SUMMARY OF OPERATIONS FOR THE WEEK ENDING 21-4-18

The following is a summary of work carried out at AKABA during the week ending 21-4-18. Operations at advanced aerodrome at Decie are not included as a separate report on these operations is being sent as soon as possible.

WORKSHOPS. On the 15th 120 h.p. Beardmore engine W.D. 1301 was run up on test bench and found O.K.

On the 16th this engine was fitted into a Martinsyde A.3957.

On the 17th one of the Le Rhone engines was cleaned ready to put into a Nieuport and on the 18th work on a 120 h.p. Beardmore W.D. 2408 was continued and Le Rhone engine Makers' No. 50192 was dismantled. On the 19th, 20th and 21st work on these two engines was continued.

M.T. One car was at advanced landing group throughout the week and one car made one journey to DECIE and back (90 miles) daily.

Crossley tender No. L.C.46 undergoing complete overhaul.

Remaining tender and 'Ford' van transported water and supplies to camp at AKABA.

RIGGING Martinsyde A. 1605: front wing bar removed and new one fitted, tail-skid and housing complete removed and new one fitted, fuselage trued up and re-covered.

Nieuport Scout No. 1566: lower port plane fitted and machine trued up.

Nieuport Scout No. 1645: machines assembled and ready for test.

GENERAL Photographic dark room made light-tight and fitted with sink, tables arid ventilators. 15 negatives were dealt with and 45 prints taken.

Instrument repairers' workshop built.

60 20 lb bombs were received per S.S. 'Burolos'

Second Transport Shed built.

During the week an Indian Army Machine Gun Instructor brought his class up to the aerodrome for instruction on the Maxim and Lewis Guns belonging to 'X' Flight which were lent him for the purpose.

FLIGHTS On 14th Nieuport Scout B. 1566 was tested and found to be flying left wing low and engine running roughly. This machine was tested again on 16th but was still flying left wing low and tail packing pieces had not been fitted.

AKABA.

22-4-18

A typing error in the X Flight Report for the week ending 13 April 1918 was signed off by Capt. Furness-Williams in Akaba with an erroneous date, 14-3-18 at the bottom of the document. At first glance it looks as if he was using the new name Royal Air Force ahead of the official date. The report for the week ending 31 March 1918 was, however, signed off on 1 April as the RFC.

X FLIGHT REPORT

The 'Report on co-operation with British and Arab troops in attack on MA'AN, WADI RETMAM, TEL EL SNANM, RAMLER and MUDHAWARA (Hedjax Railway)' was signed by Capt. F.M. Furness-Williams in Ma'an for the Week ending 1 May 1918.

Akaba, Decie and Gueira were all mentioned in this lengthy report.

Lawrence arrived in car on 19/4/18 to say that the ground attack on MA'AN had failed.

Designed matting hangar to take six machines.

An entry dated 19-4-18 read:

> The following message was dropped on Headquarters at about 1700:- 'Some camels and men hidden behind "EB" number about 50, Whether hostile or friendly not known.'

Among other matters reported for 21 April 1918:

> At 2400 Lt. Col. Lawrence arrived by 'Ford' car from MUDHAWARA and reported that on the 20th the train reported by R.A.F. reconnaissance had arrived from TEBUE with 2 Austrian howitzers.

In that report Furness-Williams made an uncharacteristic plea. He must have felt desperate.

> If operations are to continue in this Country we must have a better machine than the Martinsyde and a machine with a reliable engine. I would not suggest the R.A.F. engine, for you will note that we have had quite a number of cracked cylnders although the greatest care has been taken. Some of the days the circulating water in the Martinsyde showed a temperature of between 90 and 95 degs. You will appreciate the fact that apart from the damage to engine this temperature will cause, the pilot has been made very uncomfortable and the heat from the engine has made him quite sick and exhausted by the end of his flight.

There is more information about captive officers.

> I could not get any information from the Turkish officers prisoners except that our bombing had had a great moral effect on them and quite a number of their troops, including Aly Asman had run into our lines when machines were over. 2/Lieut. Iz-el-Din asked me to drop following note on our next raid to MUDHA ARA: 'O.C. MUDHARARA, We are in good health. We remained one night in the British flying camp where we were comfortable with best respect we met. Our compliments to our comrades. 2nd/Lt. Iz-el-Din, Warrant Officer-Aly Osman.'

An advanced aerodrome was operating some 20 miles from Gueira, in Decie, and it must have been there where George watched a 'hamlas', a procession of camels, horses and people, arriving on the landing ground. He wrote:

> A 'hamlas', a procession of camels, horses and people, of Arabs arrived.

George was impressed.

> From early morning, both Aquaba and Decie aircraft had been busy all day and a couple of Aquaba machines had returned to our drome in the afternoon to concentrate their efforts from there. There was no sign of any Arabs in the

direction of the Nagab range of hills in direct line with our aircraft attacks but at about four o' clock in the afternoon we saw some coming away from Mudowwara along a narrow Wadi that could not be seen from our position. They looked as if they were emerging from behind a brown curtain. All our aircraft were away from the drome and busy over Mudowwara, so my four mechanics and I were able to watch them. It was a sight the film operator would have enjoyed as it was a hot day with clear blue skies. The sunburnt brown hills were surrounded by green scrub at the base of the escarpment. At first only a handful of Arabs appeared then gradually the numbers increased as Arabs on horses and camels approached at a steady walk across the mudflat towards our position. A couple of our machines landed, we filled up and they took off again towards Mudowwara. Meanwhile while the procession increased in numbers as some came out the hills turning towards Gueira. The Arab force was half the distance between us and the hills when our machines started to land. The trailing party of Arabs was emerging from the narrow Wadi with our back up armoured cars taking up the rear. They were gradually filling up our aircraft parking place just near to the four foot sand dunes covered with scrub, about fifty yards from the only muddy pool of water in the area. The pool, like a drain sump, being a little lower than the flat where the small channels of rain water at some time in the past had flowed.

It was a memorable and picturesque sight as camels, horses and foot soldiers straggled over. Quite suddenly, a group began racing each other on camels and horses with full gusto in a competition to be first at the water hole.

Our pilots, now worried that they would not be able to land among the crowds of visitors, decided to get down quickly before the landing ground was totally obstructed. I was worried in case one of the pilots would end the day disastrously but fortunately all went well. The last two machines were the Martinsydes which arrived later in the day to keep an eye on the enemy.

If the Turks had sent a couple of aircraft in that day, they would have had some wonderful targets and caused havoc. By dusk, both the Arabs and the aircraft were fully exposed but the enemy did not follow up. Our machines with their twenty and one hundred-pound bombs must have done much damage to the enemy at Mudowwara. The pilots had gone into the attack at a very low altitudes resulting in two BEs being damaged by rifle fire. Their centre sections had been damaged and after consultation since it was decided to fly one back and to have a replacement centre section sent out to us for the other one. After the two pilots of the damaged machines said they would chance flying them into Aquaba, Furness-Williams, Lieutenant Makins and I eventually agreed that either Lt. Divers or Oldfield would fly one machine into Aquaba while Lt. Makins would stay with the machine that we could repair. Williams said, 'I can't have you Makins taking a risk and losing you and your machine. Anyway will have your Lewis gun if required.'

It looked as if Furness-Williams had decided to accompany Divers to Aquaba for George wrote:

> Williams said, 'We will return in the early morning, at dawn, with bombs. We'll circle over and fire a Verey light and Makins will reply, All well. If any counter attack should have happened while we were away, we will not land but go straight into action.'

TURKISH PRISONERS WELCOMED THEIR STAY

> We were left the BE and we settled down for the evening with our visiting Arab friends as they were busy giving camels and horses refreshers from the muddy-looking water nearby. They then left about fourteen Turkish prisoners on our hands, near our two bell tents.
>
> All had settled down for a rest. No campfires were lit and there was no chance of any glimmering cigarettes because the Arabs did not smoke! Besides we were completely out of cigs ourselves. It was about midnight when we settled down for it was too chilly at night to lounge about outside.
>
> We were woken up at about four the following morning. To our surprise not an Arab could be seen. All our Arab visitors had departed during the night, back to go to Gueira. No doubt to blow up the railway track between Mudowwara and Maan. But they had left the prisoners with us! Some were awake and the others were sleeping on the sand near our tents. In fact, after doing us all in while we slept, they could have been back in their own lines at Mudowwara within hours! I suppose they thought it was better to be alive and safe than to take a chance of being found by any Arabs or, on the other hand, they may have been unaware that Mudowwara was still held by their army.

X FLIGHT REPORT

The X Flight, Royal Air Force: Summary of Operations for the week ending 5 May 1918 was signed by Furness-Williams in Akaba.

> Lt. Dutton arrived on an R.E. 8 from Palestine Front with Lt. Col. Lawrence.

The Royal Aircraft Factory R.E.8, nicknamed 'The Harry Tate', a Scottish comedian, was a two-seater biplane reconnaissance and bomber with a four-blade propeller. It was a replacement for the B.E.2 but was actually more difficult to handle. By November 1918 it was regarded as obsolete. On this occasion it was being used as a taxi for Lawrence.

X FLIGHT REPORT

The X Flight, Royal Air Force: Summary of Operations for the week ending 11 May 1918 was signed by Furness-Williams in Akaba.

Under the heading Motor Transport the report said:

> On the 4th a Crossley tender took Lt. Col. Lawrence to NAGB EL ESHTAR and remained the night with him there.

Under the heading the report stated:

> On the 5th Lieut. Dutton with Lt. Col. Lawrence as passenger, returned to Palestine on his R.E.8 and a B.E.2e was tested.

George recalls:

> On the day before Captain Williams left us to return to Aquaba after a very busy morning from four o' clock till midday and after our machines had been inspected and refuelled ready for an afternoon of flying, he said, 'Hynes we are not flying this afternoon and we pilots are going to have a nap this afternoon. Give the boys some ammunition and go out and enjoy yourselves with some rifle practice.'
>
> We did, with 50 rounds of rifle ammo and 24 rounds of a revolver ammo and went off in the direction south and where there seemed much greener scrub in the distance looking very green away from the mud flat and it was the first time I had seen any sign of animal life other than desert dogs and rats.
>
> This area gave us some amusement in trying to shoot at some small animals we had disturbed firing at the scrub and [it] surprised us to see a large number of gazelles were so near as we never had a chance to wander away from our parking place for daylight was available only for our flying duties.

X FLIGHT REPORT

The X Flight Report for the week ending 19 May 1918 was signed by Siddons as Capt. and CO of the Flight in Akaba.

> On the 16/5/18 Capt. F.H. Furness-Williams proceeded to Egypt, by sea, and Lieut. V.D. Siddons assumed command of the Flight.

The report mentioned an attack on the railway station at Tel es Sham north of Mudowarra on 12 May 1918. Arabs supported by armoured cars charged in to destroy large stretches of railway line between Ma'an and Mudowarra.

On 16 May 1918 Siddons and Junor were checking the suitability of Gueira as a permanent advanced drome. Akaba to Decie is about 50 miles.

According to an internet source:

> 1 Squadron Australian Air Force, had served as Lawrence of Arabia's taxi on several occasions, on the 16th of May, 1918, Ross Smith flew Lawrence to Fiesel's Army.[36]

George mentions the advanced drome.

> We carried on from Decie through May and June for it was in May that Furness-Williams returned to Aquaba and Lieutenant Siddons took charge of us bringing news that Williams had been a recalled to headquarters. Another very active commanding officer stayed for about seven months. Our flight had been expanded and we had that 'pep' which I saw in their Sinai advance. Our complement of officers had included Freeman, Wilberforce, Grant, Makins, Tipton and Captain Dempsey, the one who always asked me to put a couple more 20 pound bombs in his cockpit as extras. He often returned from raids with a couple of tins of bully beef missing from his emergency rations because he liked to throw a couple overboard as much to say, 'Share this among you!' A tin of bully could become a deadly weapon if it hit someone in the trenches below.

The Dempsey George mentioned was probably Captain J.A.D. Dempsey of the Australian Air Force who was one of two pilots, who, with 1st Air Mechanic Doig, flew a modified Martinsyde along the surface of the Dead Sea! The wings and tail had been stripped from an obsolescent Martinsyde bomber and floats had been fitted in place of those wings. It then became a fast catamaran nicknamed 'Mimi' which had her first outing on 1 March 1917. When in hot pursuit of a Turkish boat, the pilot stood up on his seat and opened fire with a Lewis gun. It had a really awesome psychological effect upon its quarry if not much else!

May/June 1918

Kader and his escort tribe return from the Turks

George recounts:

> The next day we received word that Williams had been recalled to headquarters and Lieutenant Siddons would take over. A few weeks later both he and Junor were promoted captains. We continued here at Decie till June with the usual operations but in May we had a received word from Captain Siddons that an attempt would be made to dislodge us, four aircraft and pilots and eight mechanics, from our position.
>
> At Decie we had received a message, thought to have come from Lawrence, that a tribe which had broken away from Feisal's army had gone over to supporting the Turks and was making its way over from the direction of Mudowwara, through the narrow wadi through which we had seen Arabs retiring a couple of months earlier with a number of the prisoners after their attack on a Mudowwara. The warning came to us around midday.
>
> This was the first time we had our motorcycle dispatch rider so Siddons sent him with a message asking for some armoured cars from Gueira. At this

time Siddons was the only pilot with us. Siddons then gave me instructions to alert the boys of our party, six of them at that time, telling them to show no signs of suspecting the Arabs if approached by them but to be extra careful. Not knowing the area, the dispatch rider had difficulties getting through to Gueira speedily so we had to plan.

When the tribe appeared our chaps were to carry on with their usual duties and to rest on their beds in the hangars when every machine had been completed ready for any emergency call. Rifles and revolvers were made ready in case Kader and his tribe tried to remove us.

After consultation with Siddons I gave the chaps instructions to rest in their beds but to stay alert telling them that our despatch rider Symmonds has gone off to Gueira for armoured car support.

We saw the advance party coming from the Turkish positions, a large range of hills, in twos and threes then about 20 followed by the main party on foot, horse and camel.

About two thirty in the afternoon Kader and his tribe were seen coming from the Turkish positions, that is from the hills bordering Mudowwara. They were about three miles away entering the wadi in a direct line towards our hangar which lay under the shadow of the large rocky hill that overlooked our position. I drew that to the attention of Captain Siddons and the six mechanics.

According to George, Kader often showed his hatred of the infidel. During the revolt he moved freely about the desert paid secretly by the Turks to cause trouble where he could.

George continues:

They were given a Lewis gun taken off a machine together with drums of ammo while I patrolled in front of the hangar talking either to Siddons or a mechanic. All was ready in case of trouble for we heard that two Arabs had been killed, murdered as they entered the wadi. It was about four thirty when they reached our area. There were about one hundred and fifty of them on camels with a mountain gun set up on a camel's back. They moved towards the end of the hill to camp and moving like a ghostly army.

Before dusk, first one Arab then another came over to our matting-covered hangars. We salaamed and they responded but we carried on normally without arousing suspicion but feeling tense and alert. Our only weapons, small arms, our Webley revolvers always to hand. The Arabs wandered back to the main body but as darkness fell on this Arabian soil anything could happen quite suddenly.

I had told two mechanics to take up positions on our right and two mechanics on the left of the hangar about fifty yards from each end of our 'hide out'. They were told not to hesitate if any attempt was made on the camp. For immediate support, Siddons and I, with four mechanics stayed close to the remaining Lewis guns, changing guard every few hours to avoid strain. These positions were protected by green scrub from which we were able to keep a good lookout without detection.

About midnight, two of the armoured cars arrived, taking up positions and relieving our men from their guard duties. It was very demanding work for a small party of seven for it was not till almost one in the morning that the two armoured cars arrived. The NCO in charge jumped out of a car, 'We will take up positions. You and the boys can get your heads down.'

It was a relief for us to get a nap before preparing the machines to take to the air at about four in the morning, our usual early morning start for operations. Siddons wanted his machine to take to the air at dawn four o' clock so we went off to sleep immediately.

Captain Siddons took his aircraft up at four a.m. with five bombs aboard but on his way he flew behind the rock to drop a message advising the tribe to move to a more comfortable position. Next day, he flew over their positions with a message dropped to them in a message bag and that was the end of any such plan that they may have had to demolish us during the night. The tribe did move on but this time to Feisal's army.

I heard no further news of where they had gone and they most likely decided it better to rejoin Lawrence and Feisal's army at Gueira and our work went on without any further disturbances. There were no roads. We emptied the distilled water from our only Beardmore engine during the night and kept it ready for replacement. Here water was more valuable than gold. Between 10 a.m. and 6.30 p.m. we endured a scorching sun and that was followed by freezing temperatures at night. We slept in two bell tents each covered during sleep by two blankets and greatcoats.

In *Revolt in the Desert*, Lawrence actually mentioned receiving a telegram from Colonel Bremond saying that Kader was in the pay of the Turks.

X Flight Report

The X Flight, Royal Air Force, Report for the week ending 25 May 1918 was signed by Capt. V.D. Siddons in Akaba.

In this report Siddons, with cool detachment, recounts a flying phenomenon.

On the 22nd 2/Lt. Latham flew to AKABA and 2/Lt Junor & Divers left DECIE to do a photographic reconnaissance of JURF and although both machines were giving full revs. they remained practically stationary over JURF and lost 2000' in height with the consequence that one machine was badly shot about by M.G. fire and the flight which had previously been done from AKABA in 3 hours 35 mins. in a B.E. 2E, on this occasion took 3 hours 50 mins.

On the 25th Capt. Siddons with Lt. Col. Lawrence in a B.E.2E and 2/Lts. Makins & Oldfield in Martinsydes did a reconnaissance of MUDAWARA, the B.E.2E afterwards returning to AKABA while the Martinsydes landed again at DECIE.

(In June 1918, George wrote a letter to his brother James Edward Hynes who was then a POW in Germany in an attempt to bolster his morale.)

MODIFICATIONS TO THE AERIAL GUNS

Ground and air crews used their skills and ingenuity in the field, modifying and adapting equipment to suit perceived purposes. An entry in a report by Siddons in June 1918 refers.

On 1 June 1918, Siddons wrote:

A B.E.2e.3681, was fitted with gun for firing at troops on the ground also with Pilot's gun for firing over centre section. As a rule the ground gun will be carried during a bomb raid and the upward firing gun when this machine is used single-seater for photographs or reconnaissance.

George also described modifications made by the mechanics.

I was detailed to work with Pound who was a marine engineer like myself. He worked on engines and on gun maintenance especially on the modifications we made on our Enfield rifles for better desert use. We did that by stripping off much of the barrel to reduce weight so making it easier for Lawrence and his warriors to carry out advanced operations where the mean carrying load was important and in such terrible heat.

Another advantage gained from our modifications was that they helped to keep the barrel cooler in action. We only left sufficient to grip the rifle with the left hand, as Jones and I did with the Lewis gun, by removing the aluminium radiator for use of the gun on aircraft. Lawrence also used the same modified Lewis gun on his camel. Our modified weapons made them easier to use when attacking the enemy from cover and easier to carry on long journeys.

CANVAS HANGARS

George continues:

Our flight had four of the original aircraft that had first arrived in Egypt. When not flying they were housed in the canvas hangars which our mechanics also used as their living quarters. A few mechanics lived in tents while others made their homes in aeroplane cases! Our pilots lived on the house ship, SS *Kaheira*, British administration headquarters, when not flying.

When not working on the kites in the evenings we just lounged about listening to the howling of the desert dogs. We got so fed up with them that we would loose off a few shots into the darkness to chase them away.

June 1918

Thoughts about killing the German commander

George recounts:

> On one occasion, in June, Captain Siddons received a message from Lawrence that General Falkenhayne, the German commander, was to pay a visit by air to Maan at the end of May, in an attempt to boost Turkish morale. Our flight commander decided to do what he could to prevent the visit. Our complement was then six mechanics, four Martinsyde Scouts and one Nieuport Scout fighter.

Falkenhayne had been largely responsible for saving the Turks at Dardanelles. The main Turkish front at this time was in Mesopotamia where the German-led force was under the command of the former Chief of General Staff who had led at Verdun, Erich von Falkenhayne.

X Flight Report

The X Flight, Royal Air Force, Report for the week ending 8 June 1918 was signed by Capt. V.D. Siddons in Akaba and reported on activities in Decie and Akaba.

Makins was temporarily in charge at Decie.

Siddons quotes a letter received at 1500 on 6 June at Decie.

> Information has been received through deserters that on 7th (tomorrow) two aeroplanes are coming to MA'AN from AMMAN with an officer of high rank. Everyone in MA'AN has been ordered to parade on his arrival and Major Maynard thinks you might be able to add to his welcome. (Sgd.) R.J. JILMAN. Capt. O.C. H.A.C.B.

Of course, the message referred to Falkenhayne. Ma'an and Amman were both in enemy territory.

George recalls:

> Siddons sent Junor up in a Nieuport Scout Fighter with orders to fly at a high altitude to pounce on Falkenhayne's aircraft and prevent him reaching Ma'an. We waited anxiously for the return of Junor with the good news that the general had received a death warrant. Junor was, however, disappointed and robbed of his victim for the general did not fly in. He must have been warned that it was wiser to cancel his visit.

The report states:

> On the 7th Lt. Makins and 2/Lt. Oldfield on Martinsydes from DECIE and Capt. Siddons on Nieuport Scout from AKABA met over MA'AN and

patrolled north of it from 0515 to 0745 the Martinsydes for the whole of the time and the Nieuport Scout for three quarters of an hour.

X FLIGHT REPORT

The X Flight, Royal Air Force: Summary of Operations for the week ending 15 June 1918 was handwritten and signed by Siddons in Gueira. Siddons stated that on:

> 13th June, Flight headquarters were moved to GUEIRA from DECIE and AKABA. Advance party for pitching camp etc. prior to removal of Flight and in future AKABA will be used only as an Equipment Base.
>
> Trouble was experienced in obtaining sufficient water at GUEIRA owing to (1) inadequacy of supply and (2) insufficient camels for drawing the water when there was any. The matter has been taken up with O.C. Troops and it is hoped that a satisfactory solution will be found. If, however, no help is received in the way of camels it will be impossible to maintain the Flight at GUEIRA and it will move from DECIE to AKABA.

X FLIGHT REPORT

The X Flight, Royal Air Force: Summary of Operations for the week ending 22 June 1918 was handwritten and signed by Siddons in Gueira although Lt Makins had been left in command there during the week.

On 22 June, 1918, Gueira became the Flight's Headquarters.

The ground attack on Mudwarra had been delayed until 28th June. Half of the matting hangar in Decie was pulled down for use in Gueira. Modifications were made to telegraph poles. Two water filters were dismantled at Akaba and re-installed in Gueira together with their pumps. Eighteen camels with personnel arrived at Gueira from Abulisan in order to draw water for the RAF. Twenty ELC (Egyptian Labour Corps) arrived by road from Akaba. Only those doing guard duties stayed on the advanced drome.

Gueira was a place Lawrence delighted in:

> We rejoiced when at last we were able to escape into the clean, fresh hills about Gueira. The early winter gave us days hot and sunny, or days overcast, with clouds massed about the head of the plateau nine miles away, where Maulud was keeping his watch in the mist and rain. The evenings held just enough of chill to add delightful value to a thick cloak and a fire.[37]
>
> From Gueira we marched down Wadi Itm to Kethira (18 miles) where we overran a Turkish post of about seventy infantry and fifty mounted men, taking most of them prisoners, and thence we went on to near Khadra, at the old stone dam in Wadi Itm (15 miles), where we came into contact with the garrison (300 men) of Akaba.[38]

Nieuport Scouts were in regular, almost daily, use by Divers and Junor. Regular bombing was carried out. In fact seldom a day went by during the whole of X Flight's service that they did not take part in bombing and reconnaissance missions. For example on 16 June 2/Lt Grant on a BE2e took seventeen photographs of Ma'an and Lt Junor who escorted him on a BE12 dropped two 100-pounders and two 20-pounders. On 22 June, thirty aerial photographs of Ma'an were taken.

Decie, with three hangars, was in use as an advanced landing ground.

The story told here by George probably refers to Gueira before the water tanks arrived.

Here, I take the opportunity, to tell of an incident on the following day. It illustrates an Arab's appreciation of our company for a snack, a drink and a smoke at a campfire while we waited for supplies to repair aircraft and to replenish our drinking water; all used up the previous day. Realising that we were out of water, Mahmoud, keeper of Lawrence's camel Ghazala showed his courtesy by offering us milk from Ghazala who then had a foal, new born after the attack on Mudowwara.

As we could not replace the centre section of our BE until the machine arrived by road transport, Lieutenant Makins, Wheeler, New and myself sat down at our fire, having a drink of tea and chatting about home. Sitting with the tea made from the dirty muddy water from which the Arabs and their animals had drunk the previous day. Mahmoud joined us and sat at our fire.

We received him in the customary Arab way, with hospitality, giving him some biscuits, a piece of cheese and a drink of tea. We continued chatting while Mahmoud sat with a deep penetrating look, asking no questions for about an hour.

To show his gratitude, he rose and indicated that we should follow him. Having exchanged a few words with him, Makins told us, 'Bring your billy cans. Our friend has some milk to give us.'

We got our cans and followed over the thick scrub covered ground to a place about 300 yards from our camp. There to our amazement was the camel and its foal. I didn't fancy camel milk but when I approached Mahmoud took my tin, stepped behind the camel and began milking it with the foal standing nearby.

He filled the tin with hot milk full of large frothy bubbles and handed it to me. I was not keen but before I could make any attempt to refuse Makins told me that such a refusal would have broken an unwritten law of the desert. 'Drink it up Hynes! It is good stuff!'

I plucked up courage and drank with the froth bubbling in front of my eyes and the smell penetrating my nostrils like a fish stall.

After gulping about half a tin I passed it on to Makins. He drank and passed on to Wheeler. The Arab filled it up again and passed it over with a smile of pleasure asking us to take it back with us. He then turned to the foal and led it to its mother for its feed. I did hear later that the foal had died even though it had seemed so sturdy standing about three feet high to its small hump.

Ghazala was a very large animal and stood much taller than I had seen any other. It looked healthy and well cared for with a clean looking coat of woolly hair rather lighter than the ordinary beast of its type. I wondered if it was free of syphilis as we young men had been told that camels were prone to such a malady and I hoped I had not been silly in taking that drink. I hoped that the Arabs knew how to judge a healthy beast for I have never been affected by illness arriving in from Arabia classified as A1, physically fit. I later returned to Blighty without any tropical ailments except for brown spot that remained with me. I once asked a surgeon what it was but his reply was. 'I have no idea!' It was about the size of a sixpence.

There was no other Arab in the vicinity and I surmised that arrangements would have to be made at the base to transport the foal by motor. There was really no way to look after it among these desert scrubs. Mahmoud might have to make a slow journey to Gueira or to Aquaba with the foal. We continued to use our 'sump' water that was like the colour of tea with the milk added. We boiled it in our large dixie and carefully poured it onto our tea ration after the sand grains had settled down. We expected the camel milk to make it seem more palatable.

Shortly after the capture of Akaba by Lawrence and the Arabs, Nasi sold the pedigree Ghazala to Lawrence at a meeting in Gueira. Ownership of that particular beast brought great honour among the Howeitat tribe.

Lawrence wrote an interesting piece about his camel.

I was on my Ghazala, the old grandmother camel, now again magnificently fit. Her foal had lately died, and Abdulla, who rode next me, had skinned the little carcase, and carried the dry pelt behind his saddle, like a crupper piece. We started well, thanks to the Zaagi's chanting, but after an hour Ghazala lifted her head high, and began to pace uneasily, picking up her feet like a sword-dancer. I tried to urge her: but Abdulla dashed alongside me, swept his cloak about him, and sprang from his saddle, calf's skin in hand. He alighted with a splash of gravel in front of Ghazala, who had come to a standstill, gently moaning. On the ground before her he spread the little hide, and drew her head down to it. She stopped crying, shuffled its dryness thrice with her lips; then again lifted her head and, with a whimper, strode forward. Several times in the day this happened; but afterwards she seemed to forget. At Gueira, Siddons had an aeroplane waiting. Nuri Shaalan and Feisal wanted me at once in Jefer. The air was thin and bumpy, so that we hardly scraped over the crest of Shtar. I sat wondering if we would crash, almost hoping it. I felt sure Nuri was about to claim fulfilment of our dishonourable half-bargain, whose execution seemed more impure than its thought. Death in the air would be a clean escape; yet I scarcely hoped it, not from fear, for I was too tired to be much afraid: nor from scruple, for our lives seemed to me absolutely our own, to keep or give away: but from habit, for lately I had risked myself only when it seemed profitable to our cause.[39]

GEORGE FLIES ON A MISSION WITH SIDDONS

George wrote about flying on a mission with Siddons.

> After we had been there about two weeks, Lieutenant Siddons told me to obtain a funnel and a few tools and to make sure that the aircraft had an extra supply of bully beef and water bottles filled to full capacity. I was to be ready to accompany him on a special mission.

V.D. Siddons joined the Territorials, the Northamptonshire Yeomanry, three years before the outbreak of the First World War when he was training to be a Methodist Minister.

At the outbreak of war he went with the 8th Division earning the 1914 Star with Aug–Nov clasp. He was commissioned and after nine months in France he was sent to the Middle East with the Northamptonshires. He transferred to the RFC and qualified as a pilot. On the Sinai Front, he was the first to take photographs of Gaza from the air.

He joined C Flight of No. 14 Squadron RFC in the Hejaz, where he served for two years, the last six months of which he commanded the X Flight. He was awarded the DFC, was Mentioned in Despatches and was also awarded the Order of Al Nahda. His 1916 diary and his Army Book 136 (Log Book) mentions acting as a pilot for Lawrence of Arabia, as does Lawrence himself in *Seven Pillars of Wisdom*.

George continues:

> At about two o'clock in the afternoon with our machine all ready, Lieutenant Siddons arrived with full instructions. 'Take this message bag. We are going to track down our two Crossley tenders. Keep a good look out for them and that means looking for car tracks to pick up their whereabouts.'
>
> 'When you spot the Crossleys, let me know and when I tell you to drop the message bag, do that and also fire a Verey light, colour white. The cars have to be prevented from completing their journey. They must return to prevent them being ambushed by the Turks.'
>
> I put on my Arab head dress which made a good flying helmet. Only pilots were supplied with RFC flying helmets and Siddons never wore anything other than his own helmet. Some of the pilots did use Arab headdress but not him. We flew off in the direction of Medina.

Medina is a city in western Saudi Arabia, north of Mecca. Mohammed's tomb is to be found there. Historically, it began as an oasis settled by Jews in about AD 135.

Muhammad, the Prophet fled from Mecca to Medina in 622 AD. The town served as capital of the Islamic state until 661; there then followed a long period of Ottoman occupation.

ACTION NEAR EL WEJH

George recounts:

> Siddons had to climb for most of the journey as we were approaching hills of about ten thousand feet. The ones that always stood out very clearly in the blazing heat when we were travelling by ship and when ashore at El Wejh. We passed over the large soft dry sand hills that even the four footed ships of the desert would instinctively never attempt to tread on.
>
> We had flown for over two hours without seeing any sign of animal or man let alone car tracks. Siddons then circled over a large piece of flat ground shaped like the inside of a large bowl with solid rock in the centre.
>
> Much to my surprise we landed there where Siddons told me we would settle for the night. Pointing over to one side of the flat, he said, 'There is petrol and oil stored here with a few biscuits and a tin of bully. I'll fetch the petrol over while you check the machine over ready to fill the tank.' We did that and with our task completed we were ready take off for the next flight.
>
> Siddons had brought along a large two and a half size tin of apricots and a small 'ship-made' Vienna style loaf, the only one I had ever seen in the whole of my time in Arabia. We sat on the sand having our evening meal comprising the warm sloppy contents of a tin of bully, our shares of the loaf and some of the apricots, all of which we finished the next morning.
>
> Dusk was rapidly approaching when we finished so we lounged about until about half past seven o' clock when Siddons pulled out a sealed envelope and passed it over to me with the instruction. 'Put this away!'
>
> I put it inside my shirt, close to my skin.
>
> 'Keep a good look out for two Arabs and when they arrive and approach you, give them the envelope. But make certain they have come for this purpose.'
>
> 'You will do two hours' duty on guard, while I am having two hours' sleep, eight till ten o' clock. Wake me up and then you can have your two hours' sleep. We will repeat the same duty until dawn when after you have done the usual check ups we will take to the air at about a four thirty.' I agreed and Siddons got down just under the starboard wing and I rested against the aircraft keeping as a good lookout as I could in a night so black that I could see no further than about ten yards.
>
> During my watch in this small oasis walled in by hills, with no breeze and the very hot stifling atmosphere with one hell of a thirst creeping up on me I thought over and over again about my favourite acid drops to moisten my tongue.

Siddons had emphasised the need to save the water in the five bottles we had left. We had drunk one of them at our meal. I realised only too well then why all our aircraft carried four bottles each when on operations. They were there to keep the pilots alive and to get them to get them back to their drome after being forced down. In those circumstances water was worth more than all the gold in the world.

I decided to patrol around the machine to keep the blood circulating and to stop the tendency to doze. The heat was terrific and I finally had to have a swig from a bottle for my mouth felt dry and nature was conquering my will.

I soon discovered that tasting water brought on a strong urge to drink more and keep on drinking but I fought the urge and tried to concentrate, peering into the darkness waiting for our friends to arrive. The temperature must have been a hundred degrees so I was tempted. I sipped and sipped and by the time I had to wake Siddons I had very nearly drunk the remainder of the bottle.

Suddenly, within yards, two figures in white appeared so silently that my hand reached for my revolver. They saluted me in true Arab fashion, hand to forehead and to the breast then a slight body bow.

I returned their salutation and pulling out the envelope I passed it to one of them who was about my own age, then twenty-one. A smile broke out on his clean-cut handsome Arab features. Both were dressed in white garments but without cloaks. They were armed with the usual belted ammo that would do them justice in action in these hills.

They both bowed and slipped away like ghostly figures into the curtain of darkness surrounding us. The hand over had been satisfactorily completed. On the rest of my watch I pondered about these Arabs with their wonderful personalities. They were friends who could be trusted to guard you safely without cutting your throat or robbing you. I glanced at the aircraft watch and seeing that Siddons was in a deep sleep I decided to give him an extra fifteen minutes. When I did wake him I told him the message was now on its way. I soon had my head down but when awakened I felt as if I had only had a few minutes doze.

We changed places again having four hours sleep each and two on guard. As daylight showed we did not trouble to have breakfast, taking to the air at about four thirty to continue our search for the two cars. After about one and half-hours flying we came across them when the two men dashed out of a small clump of palm trees where they had sheltered for the night.

Siddons circled round and I dropped the message bag. They signalled back with their Verey light and we turned for El Wejh. I dozed off in the machine after having a few bites from the remainder of the loaf but I was suddenly woken up when Siddons knocked on the top of my cockpit. He pointed over the Red Sea on the fringe of the coastline on our port side and there I saw the most beautiful sight that I had ever seen, a large cloud in beautiful colours like a mass of stationary candyfloss sprinkled with all the colours of the rainbow.

Once again I fell asleep, remembering nothing until I was roused by Toby Wheeler and Siddons and a couple of other boys who [were] laughing their heads off. 'Come on George! Don't you want some breakfast?'

Now awake I realised that I had had at least another hour's sound sleep in the aircraft on the trip back to El Wejh. It also dawned on me why a certain pilot when flying always took a book with him to read on this way out from Aquaba.

It was a strain flying over Arabian desert lands with a scorching sun overhead and the hot fumes from the engine exhaust breather pipes that allowed the hot gases from the crankcase to flow out. The vapours had a tendency to upset the balance of the stomach. It was monotonous travelling at 80 mph, at about five or more thousand feet with the sensation that we were only crawling along especially on an empty stomach.

George mentioned the high levels of secrecy which were maintained.

Newcombe and Hornby assisted the Arabs with their attacks on the railways but little 'intelligence' about forthcoming attacks ever got through to the Turks despite their air reconnaissance and the willingness for some Arabs to sell information to one side or the other!

Seldom could the enemy machines stand up to the conditions that for example X Flight had to put up with all the time. That spoke well of the bravery of the Allied pilots flying inferior machines and the skills of the mechanics who kept them in the air. For example, George mentioned that on at least one occasion, X Flight had heard that two German and Turkish aircraft had crashed in Medina with pilots killed.

JUNE 1918

WATER TABLETS USED ON ADVANCED DROMES

George recalls:

Dr Marshall supplied us with a bottle of disinfectant tablets to put into our well water and our 'sump water' when we had to resort to using impure water during our operations in the field.

Furness-Williams emptied his water bottles into ours the next day till our Crossley arrived with spare parts and the 20 gallon copper water container. This was for desert use on the camels.

We now occupied the hangar housing our aircraft during our advanced operations and discarded our old mudflat parking places. Just before we took over in April we had been busy bombing and carrying out constant reconnaissance. We were given a very important air engagement.

POTENTIAL ATTACKERS

However trusting of Arab allies George and his colleagues were, they had to be very wary at a time when the Turks also recruited and used local tribesmen to do their spying for them. That caution is illustrated several times by George as in this incident.

> Shortly afterwards, a month later, just before dusk, a couple of Arabs approached our hangar. I went over to a machine and pretended to settle a gun and its mounting and when they came to the front of the hangar to have a look around I nodded to them and took no further notice just as if ordinary routine was in progress.

> They returned to the tribe but showing our chaps their positions in the scrub area bordering the base of our hill. I gave instructions that they would mount guard with rifles, in two hours shifts, until the cars arrived. Having a Lewis gun, I was to keep in close contact with our chaps during any attempt to attack us. I had used the Lewis on Sinai and I was confident that Siddons and I could break any attacking sortie made on us.

> We operated out of Decie into the middle of June, keeping the Turks hemmed in by bombing raids, co-ordinating with Arab attacks above Maan and between there and Mudowwara.

> Lawrence and Allenby were now preparing for the final victory over the Turks when in June, we left Decie and returned to Aquaba. I was only there a week when I took a party of six mechanics to Gueira on a selected landing ground for [the] first time to receive our French canvas hangar, two bell tents and a marquee for the pilots. We were then stationed close to the main staff of Feisal's Arab base ready for the Northern drive.

> Junor, Divers and Makins joined us with their machines and carried out the usual bombing and reconnaissance flights. Sergeant Clements of the Royal Engineers and some Egyptian labourers also joined us with a couple of woodworkers and they set to building us a hangar similar to the one we'd had at Decie.

JULY 1918

X FLIGHT REPORT

The X Flight, Royal Air Force: Summary of Operations for the week ending 13 July 1918 was signed by Siddons in Gueira. Siddons wrote:

> Work on the aerodrome is now almost finished the surface being fairly good. The aerodrome is now L shaped being 500 yds long on one side & 350 yds

along the other. Trenches for petrol to be stored in have now been commenced. The second matting hangar is finished, but the first one to be built has had to have the roof replaced owing to the fact that the sudden winds have almost entirely destroyed the old one.

Siddons also wrote:

On the 9th 2/Lt. Oldfield & 2/Lt. Latham left to carry out topographical Reco of EL JAFAR. The Armoured Car Hqrs. at the NE end of the depression was located & several appar good landing grounds observed.

On the 13th Lt. Divers & 2/Lt. Grant on BE2E started out to bomb and rec MUDAWARA. An engine was observed in the station siding with steam up. Twelve 20lb Coopers bombs were dropped eight of which fell into the station enclosure. [Note: Cooper bombs exploded on impact.] One direct hit was reported on station building. The viaducts north of the main MUDAWARA viaduct are still in a damaged condition. Captain Siddons & 2/Lt. Hounsell with 2 O.R. in Crossley tender carried out ground reconnaissance near TEL EL SHAHM with a view to finding Advanced Landing Ground. A report will be rendered later on reasons for the reco & operations arising therefrom.

CASTOR OIL POPULAR

Castor oil was used as a lubricant in rotary aero engines because it did not dissolve in gasoline. However, during flight the castor oil was messily spewed out into the slipstream. George recalled one flight when the contents of the slipstream made him sick. On another occasion some of the Flight's castor oil supply brought about some messy consequences among the Arabs and Egyptians in the Flight's workforce! Little did they know that the oil was also an effective purgative.

George recalls:

During my work, I tried an experiment which turned out to be very amusing. We had some castor oil for use in aero engines. I decided to swallow some to clear out my system. It was the very first time I had ever taken such stuff. I opened a four gallon tin and took an army dessert spoonful. I hadn't noticed that an Egyptian labourer had been watching me, 'Berry good Johnny.' I replied 'Quaskitia!' and obliged him by giving him a spoonful too.

The next day he came to me with four more of his pals asking me for more. 'Good Johnny! Good!' pointing to his bottom. I gave them a spoonful each much to the amusement of my friends. The Egyptians departed, all smiles, pleased with this wonderful medicine.

The next day they came again with a few more people, so I thought these contributions to their welfare are getting beyond my generosity. When all were beaming with expectation, I got my enamel army cup and filled it a quarter full giving it to the leader asking, 'You like this?' He beamed repeating, 'Berry good!' and drank it with gusto as they all did.

George Hynes in Arab head dress during his service with X Flight.
(Courtesy Ellen Gannicott)

George Hynes in the middle row, five from the right, standing behind Captain Henderson and to his right Lieutenant Stafford, whilst serving with C Flight of 14 Squadron. (*Courtesy Roger Bragger*)

X Flight's camp at Akaba. *(Imperial War Museum)*

Lawrence aboard his
ship of the desert.
(Imperial War Museum)

The Emir Feisal bin Husain al-
Hashimi, the future King of Iraq.
(Imperial War Museum)

A photograph taken by
Lawrence of the Emir Feisal and
his Arab troops.
(Imperial War Museum)

First Air Mechanic Forder of X
Flight cooks a meal in the desert.
(Courtesy Barbara Rudoe)

Two of X Flight's pilots eating lunch, probably hard tack. *(Courtesy Barbara Rudoe)*

Air Mechanic Frank Birkinshaw in RFC uniform. *(Courtesy Barbara Rudoe)*

Junor's downed fighter.
(Imperial War Museum)

Six X Flight members stand
by the wreck of the
downed Rumpler.
(Courtesy Barbara Rudoe)

Lieutenant Makins of X Flight.
(Courtesy Barbara Rudoe)

A.M. Forder leaning
against a somewhat ruined
building with Arabs
sheltering within.
(Courtesy Barbara Rudoe)

An X Flight Crossley tender in difficult terrain.
(Courtesy Barbara Rudoe)

Air Mechanic Forder driving the X Flight Crossley.
(Courtesy Barbara Rudoe)

This sketch by George Hynes is thought to be of Lord Winterton cooking breakfast for Lawrence and the X Flight mechanics at an advanced landing ground. *(Courtesy Ellen Gannicott)*

Hamlas arriving at the muddy pool near X Flight's advanced landing ground sketched by George Hynes. *(Courtesy Ellen Gannicott)*

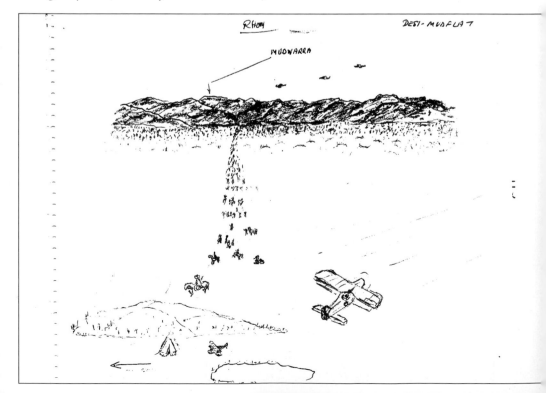

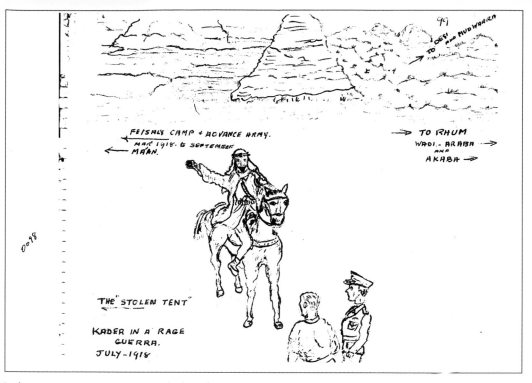

Kader in a rage accusing X Flight of stealing a tent in July 1918 as seen by George Hynes. *(Courtesy Ellen Gannicott)*

A signed photograph of T.E. Shaw on his bicycle. *(Courtesy Ellen Gannicott)*

338171 A/c Shaw
R.A.F.
Mount Batten
Plymouth.
25 · X · 32

Dear Hynes

Congratulations on George. I hope he and Mrs Hynes are flourishing. You are forging ahead in family!

I'm back in my proper place now, the motor boats all finished and running strongly. To be in camp again is like a rest cure. The hours seem so short. Just at the moment my job is to pull to bits a series of motor-boat again. It is rather a puzzle, everything being rusted solid.

Arabs had the better climate, anyway. Engines didn't rust solid in a week! Parts of our war were not so bad, I suppose, though personally I hated it.

You shall have that photo when I come across something possible: but I won't go to a photographer and be taken. There are copies of some artists' drawings that I used to have. One of those when I lay my hands on them again. No papers in camp!

Yours
TE Shaw

A letter from T.E. Shaw to George Hynes written in October 1932.
(Courtesy Ellen Gannicott)

3 Bruxxx......
Southampton

21 · XII · 33

Dear Hynes

Still there? Probably not. I'm in Southampton for the moment, building boats for the R.A.F. My proper station is at Felixstowe where I expect to be for the next fourteen months. After that I get my orange card and have to look after myself.

I hope your affairs are well. This has been a rotten year for everybody. Let's hope 1934 is a bit more prosperous. I'm afraid it won't be so in a summer though. It was like the East down here: week after week of sunshine and warmth...only.

Best wishes for .34

yours

T E Shaw

A letter from T.E.Shaw to George Hynes, written in 1933 when Shaw was in Southampton working on the development of RAF high-speed motor launches. *(Courtesy Ellen Gannicott)*

Clouds Hill,
Moreton,
Dorset.

4 St James's Square
S.W.1.

5. June. 35

Dear Mr. Hynes,

Thank you for your letter of May 20th. You will probably have seen from the papers that (just that I told them, this was got out somehow) that the piece of ... rush or grass from Akaba, X Flight, was placed with my brother's body inside the coffin.

Yours sincerely,
A.W. Lawrence

A letter written on 5 June 1935 by Lawrence's brother A.W. Lawrence to George Hynes. The letter explains that a piece of rush or grass from Akaba sent by X Flight was placed in Lawrence's coffin. (Courtesy Ellen Gannicott)

George Hynes on home leave during World War Two. *(Courtesy Ellen Gannicott)*

The 14 Squadron badge and crest. *(Courtesy 14 Sqn Historian)*

There was no queue the next day but Mahmoud came up looking very white and giving me mournful looks, shaking his head from side to side. 'What's to do, Mahmoud?'

'No souise!' he replied, shrugging his shoulders and pointing to his bottom.

'Much! Not good!' Three other workers near him, one, a black Sudanese and two Arabs looking interested. The Sudanese said, 'Too much!' He and the others and the Egyptian spoke again, 'Sh...sh...sh....' and pointed to about six men all sitting on their haunches in the sand dunes.

It dawned on the Sudanese what the trouble was and he roared laughing and shared the joke in Arabic with the Arabs and they also seeing the joke doubled up with laughter. Arabs having picked up some of our language walked over to the men in the bush, laughing and repeating, 'Sh.. Sh.. Sh..'

We met the Sudanese at Gueira as he helped Sergeant Clemence to build matting covered hangars ready for our base at Aquaba when we moved there. He was always singing and getting his workmates to chant 'Sh.. Sh..!' The only way that Sergeant Clemence could change the tune was by dropping his false teeth. The Sudanese would take fright and jump off the top and run away. Then his Egyptian workers in their turn would then have a good laugh. When Sergeant Clemence of the Royal Engineers was handling them, we christened it, Gueira's Music Hall so we did have a little fun now and then.

TRAINING FITTERS

George recalls:

I remember a British miner who joined us in Aquaba. He was one of a small number of men transferred from infantry units to strengthen our flight in 1918. He could not read or write and at sixty years of age he had volunteered to serve his king and country. Although an experienced miner he was otherwise unskilled but we trained him to become a fitter. When he stripped off his shirt to get washed it could be seen that he was scarred from head to foot. The blue scars had been caused by falls of coal since his boyhood days.

BRITISH SOLDIER MURDERED

George continues:

Some time later the one and only Briton to be killed by Arabs happened at the well in the Wadi Ithm.

One afternoon, one of the armoured cars had stopped at the well where following standing orders, the crew filled up the radiator, refilled water bottles and a copper twenty gallon container before continuing their journey from Aquaba to their base.

Corporal Bond was in charge of the armoured car that stopped to fill up and it so happened that a couple of young Arab bloods were also at the well when they arrived. The two Arabs were in some way molesting the Arab women and Corporal Bond had stepped in to protect them when one of the Arabs shot him with his rifle. Bond died instantly but no further action was taken until the matter was taken up with Feisal.

Emir Feisal sent scouts out into the hills to arrest the culprits who were caught about two weeks later. They were tried and sentenced to death. They were hung up on palm trees alive and on the words of command the whole of the Arabs in the area were given freedom to carry out the execution and it was carried out without any dissension.

Feisal's laws came into operation in ordering the execution of the two culprits at Gueira in 1918. Feisal also made a proclamation that any such act against Britishers would be dealt with by decapitation and being strung up in palm trees as a lesson to others. No other Briton was ever murdered there. Corporal Bond was buried at Aquaba in 1918, in the British sector.

OUR PILOTS ATTACK AN ENEMY MACHINE

George tells of yet another brush with the enemy.

On one particular day, Williams had returned to Aquaba and Lieutenant Siddons was left in charge with pilots, Junor and Divers. We had the three Martinsyde Scouts and the BE2C, when one afternoon we saw a Turkish machine flying at about 8,000 feet from the direction of Mudowwara over the mud flat and in the direction of Aquaba. The enemy machine continued his flight in the same direction so we expected to have a visit from him later. A quick decision was made by the three pilots to go into action.

We mechanics started up the three Scouts and the pilots made a quick take-off as the enemy machine passed out of sight and ours raced after him gaining height to go in for a kill. Our Scouts flew out of sight but then we saw the enemy machine returning in a direct line for Maan. Our pilots did not seem to have any opportunity to meet him in the air but when the three machines arrived back after about 40 minutes, the pilots were full of glee as they jumped out of their cockpits.

'Well that was a surprise for the enemy when we dived on him and forced him down with the three guns!' and Junor said, 'Yes, it was an anxious time for me trying to go in for the kill when we all wanted to make use of our bullets!'

It was the first time that I had seen Siddons so full of pleasure as he was always inclined to be rather self conscious about his status as an officer, never associating and relaxing with his mechanics at a camp fire like Williams, Makins and others.

What impressed me at the time was that each of those machines had symbols painted on the sides to their individual machines. Lt. Siddons had his engine cowling painted white with a red devil, with very grinning face complete with horns, cloven hoofs and that trident instrument of death.

That was George's version of the one reported here by Siddons himself.

X FLIGHT REPORT

The X Flight, Royal Air Force, Report for the week ending 6 July 1918 was signed by Capt. V.D. Siddons in Gueira. The report stated:

On the 1st as the three machines were landing a hostile machine was observed from the ground going S. Capt. Siddons in a Nieuport immediately took off in chase of EA but his engine cut out soon after taking off. The EA was then seen to turn N and was lost sight of. About half an hour after EA again appeared from the direction of Akaba at a great height. Capt. Siddons on a Nieuport & Lt. Makins on BE12A immediately took off in pursuit. Capt. Siddons caught up EA about 1 mile SSE of Maan and got in a burst of three, but gun jambed [sic] he then did a climbing turn, & corrected jamb & again dived on EA, but after getting off a burst of three, gun again jambed & this time could not be rectified. As BE12A could not catch EA up, both machines returned having seen EA do a good landing about 1 mile S of MAAN near the railway line. It was afterwards reported that this hostile machine dropped three light bombs near the French camp at Akaba without doing any damage. The machine was not observed at all whilst bombing as he was at such a great height, & no one at AKABA was aware that the place was being bombed.

Signed, Siddons, Capt., RAF, O.C. X Flight Royal Air Force

George recalls:

At the time it made me think of Auda who when we were on the Decie mudflat, was excitedly pressing Williams to get into the machine. Williams tried to explain that he could not agree with a suggestion made by that great Arab warrior as it was against Lawrence's advice. Nevertheless Williams did take him on a flight towards Mudowwara.

Having returned, Auda was even more excited. Williams told me what it was about. 'He wants us to allow him to lie in the bottom of the fuselage so that he can fire through a hole in the fabric and shoot at the Turks.'

It was difficult to tell him that his wish could not be granted even after we opened the side of the frame to show him the cross bracing wires that would prevent Auda carrying out his request, the privilege of using the Turks as a target practice from the air. It would not only have been dangerous to take him or even to take one of our mechanics unless he was very experienced. The limited angle of attack from the observer's cockpit could result in a gunner shooting the tail section off.

Lawrence described Auda as the 'greatest fighting man in northern Arabia'. He was a leading hero in the Arab revolt. His audacious bravery as a warrior was unforgettably displayed in the film *Lawrence of Arabia*.

George continues:

> We continued operations with Furness-Williams and about three pilots staying with us for a few days until replaced by Lieutenant Siddons. Arrangements had been made to change the pilots turn and turn about with at least one being with us on our advanced position. That way the pilots could stay in more comfortable quarters overnight on board HMS *Humber*. They could not be blamed for wanting a little comfort after a day's operations. Ground staff were often hard at work till late at night but pilots were off duty when night fell.
>
> We were confined to our duties twenty four hours a day. As an NCO I had never been able to take regular strolls to the jetty except on one occasion. That was when Wheeler and I decided to go down one night to see if we could obtain some smokes. We finished up having a smoke with a generous Arab with his hookah and tobacco leaf. Back at Decie we had a very busy time. In fact things were warming up from dawn to dusk, bombing in Mudowwara and making heavy attacks on Maan. Our four Martinsydes from Decie were brought into use for about a week co-operating with our machines from the base at Aquaba leading up to the fall of Maan railway station.

X FLIGHT REPORT

The X Flight, Royal Air Force, Report for the week ending 20 July 1918 was signed by Capt. V.D. Siddons in Gueira.

> On the 18th as a result of the reco of JURF EL DERWISH & MAAN on the 15th inst., it was decided to attack hamlas seen on the road running parallel to the railway line. Accordingly Lt. Junor on a BE12A left with 8 20 lb. Coopers Bombs. At about 2 miles N of MAAN, a hamlas of about 30 camels & 25 men was located & bombed, two direct hits being observed. Owing to an early stoppage with the ground Lewis gun, it was impossible to machine-gun them. Information was received later that 4 Turks had been killed & 5 wounded & 6 camels killed. 2/Lt. Oldfield on Nieuport did offensive patrol over MAAN.

HUNTING DESERT RATS

Some recreational activity was available at advanced dromes. George recounts:

When Junor was in camp with us, like Williams, he was always willing to join in with his ground staff. A competition was organised during the dark nights when all we could see around us were the desert rats. They seemed to be attracted to us, enjoying themselves like kangaroos these rats could jump about five feet into the air.

They were unseen in daylight but they could still be a danger to our machines during landings and because of that our party of the Egyptians were employed to fill in the rat holes during the day.

The competition was to hunt the rats and kill them. Junor promised to present a large tin of fruit to the winner. We started the attack outside our tents with each man wielding a large tent peg such as those used on the marquees. We roamed about outside of the tents making wild swipes at the rats as they jumped but managed to kill some and it was entertainment for us and for them, perhaps! Junor and his co-pilots joined in and we went all out for the prize as we never ever enjoyed the luxury of tinned fruit on our rations.

When the wooden and matting covered hangar was complete, Captain Siddons and our other pilots with machines joined us making Gueira our forward base protecting Feisal's staff and Arabs from enemy aircraft. This was all at a time when Lawrence's tactics were showing their effectiveness. More and more parties of Arabs on camels trudged it from Aquaba gathering for the big attack.

There were high hills to the north, west and east of Gueira. Rumm was almost due south; Wadi Araba, the long valley, lay across the hills to the west; Akaba was about 20 miles south-west. Feisal's camp was nearby and Auda with his tribe lived near the Hejaz railway.

KADER SHOWS UP AGAIN IN GUEIRA

George recalls:

One morning, in July, 1918, at about 5.30 a.m., I was standing on the drome with Captain Siddons. A couple of machines left to fly over the enemy positions and we were the only two on the landing ground standing about thirty feet from or tents. During our conversation I noticed an Arab on horseback about 400 yards away racing across the drome. He came straight towards us in a mad dash.

We awaited his arrival as he dashed along with his cloak flying in the slipstream, urging his horse on in that mad gallop. About six feet away from us he pulled up with a jerk in a mad rage roaring Arabic at us.

We calmly watched his clear-cut handsome dark features full of anger with arms waving about. He had no rifle with him, only a cross belt of revolver ammo and a revolver in his waist belt. A raging torrent of words poured out as, gesticulating with his right hand, he followed up with final sweep of his arm in the direction of his camp at the end of a large rocky hill that faced our drome. All that took place in about six seconds.

We were never without our webbing belt and loaded revolvers with about twelve rounds in the ammo pocket. As I faced the man I rested my right hand on my belt with thumb between belt and body so that when he swung his arm with the grenade, I slid my hand over the gun butt and kept it there in case he did throw but I did not draw it.

He stood staring me in the eyes and I him, for I had learned in my contact with the Arabs that they have a natural gift of staying silent if they do not understand our conversation. They would sit and stare as if reading your mind with those dark unflinching eyes.

His arm suddenly dropped down into his garment from which he took out a small hand grenade holding it up ready to throw at us. Just as suddenly his throwing arm stopped while held at full extent above his head. It remained poised while he looked me full in the face like a silent bronze figure for a few seconds before dropping his hand. His mood seemed to have changed in an instant. He may even have been annoyed with himself for his threatening behaviour.

With a sharp pull on the reins with his left hand he swung his horse around and dashed back the way he came.

I asked Siddons what the trouble was, he replied, 'He said someone had stolen one of his tents during the night and accused us of being the culprits.' I read later that it was Abd el Kader, the young hot-headed rebel.

AUGUST 1918

A few sentences from a summary of operations written in early August confirms the accepted use of the word 'on' rather than 'in' when referring to pilots and their aircraft – almost always 'machines'. It also confirms the fact that ground troops are strafed and bombed by both sides as well as buildings, tents, camels and such. In reports, enemy aircraft were always called EA or reported by their make e.g. Taube.

X FLIGHT REPORT

The X Flight, Royal Air Force: Summary of Operations for the week ending 3 August 1918 was signed by Siddons, probably in Gueira

> On the 1st Lt. Divers on a B.E.12A and Lieut. Sefi, and 2/Lieut. Grant on a B.E.2.E. set out to bomb MAAN. The target for bombing was the quarries lying immediately N. of the Station, this being the spot where the Garrison generally took shelter (Latter information obtained from Turkish Officer Deserter). In all 19 20lb Coopers bombs were dropped, and 732 rounds of S.A.A. [Small Arms Ammunition] fired at suitable ground targets.

On the 1st 4 E.A. (2 German, 2 Turkish) bombed the Arab camp at TAHONIE. 3 machines came rather low, bombing and machine gunning the Arabs, while one machine held off and kept rather high. The latter was thought to be a scout.

On the 4th Captain Siddons proceeded to ABU LESAL by Crossley tender and mule, and thence to TAHONIE by Ford Car. TAHONIE is about 5 miles W. of MAAN, and in the centre of the ARAB ARMY camp. A landing ground was chosen for Nieuports, it being the only possible place for a Nieuport to land for 30 miles from GUEIRA to MAAN. The Flight at present is protecting an army 30 miles from the aerodrome from bombing raids with only 2 Scout machines in the Flight.

Tahonie, was definitely in the enemy's backyard being only 5 miles from Ma'an where the Turks were entrenched but regularly bombed by X Flight, almost as a matter of routine. It is possible that Tahonie is the place later referred to as X. According to the report for the week ending 10 August 1918 Junor flying a Nieuport went at dawn on the 8th to a landing ground in Tahonie. He was so close he could almost have reached out and touched the enemy!

GEORGE REPAIRS PLANE DOWNED IN DESERT

George recalls:

Then came a flight going to the attend to the first forced landing of one of our machines after a raid on Mudowwarra. Lieutenant Junor had returned to our base reporting that Lieutenant Makins had been forced to land. After refuelling Junor's machine, I was detailed to take a few tools out to the stranded machine.

I was taken, by a very active, agile and fearless pilot, Lieutenant Junor. After we took off, he took us up the Wadi Araba for about four miles, turned towards the hills on our starboard heading directly for them. He did not attempt to gain height to fly over but instead, flew through the Wadi Ithm entering it while flying below the hilltops.

When we came close to the wall ahead he turned sharply left up the Wadi and flew a few degrees in the direction of the flat rock strewn sand dunes over Rhum in the direction of Mudowwara. He put down on the Seven Mile mud flat of Desi and taxied up to Makins' machine. [They must have been flying out of Akaba, north then turning sharply east. The Seven Mile mud flat must have been close to Tel el Shahm.]

I examined the machine and discovered a mechanical breakage of the magneto driving spindle which had sheared. So far as I know it was the only time such a thing had happened on a BE2C. I had to tell Junor that it would mean sending up a Crossley tender and trailer with some ropes and two mechanics to dismantle the machine and take it back to Aquaba.

Junor flew back to base while I prepared to do the dismantling by taking out split pins and removing propeller engine fixing bolts followed by the airframe main planes securing bolts ready for lifting off when the team arrived by midday. On his return, Lieutenant Makins also gave a hand as he had himself come the hard way having been a member of the Duke of Westminster's armoured cars when they captured Jaffa Pasha's Senussi in Libya in 1915. Lt. Slessor of our C Flight also helped. Makins was of the type like Kingsford Smith who liked to take a hand in helping the mechanics and would sit at the camp fire after flights.

We had not seen another human being during our first stay on that occasion. In fact, it was a fairly hot day with clear blue skies and very peaceful but we knew that over the other side of those hills was Mudowwara with her strong enemy patrols.

Fortunately Makins had managed to give us about one and a half miles of open ground between us and those hills. Nevertheless if the Turks had been adventurous they could have used one of their aircraft to totally smash our machines. Cavalry or camel troops could have made an attempt although we would have been able to give them a good welcome with our Lewis gun and about 500 rounds of .303 ammo.

Having made the machine ready to be dismantled quickly, Makins and I settled down to a snack of emergency rations of bully and biscuits with a wash down from one of our four water bottles from the kite. We then lounged about near our machines until nightfall.

It had become very chilly during the night and I was compelled to light a small fire behind some small sand tunes to make a warm drink of water for us. We passed the night talking until the Crossley arrived from Aquaba. We were very relieved when we saw the flickering lights of the tender's carbide headlamps just after midnight as it came in from Rhum.

They must have been on the ground a few miles west of Mudowwara with a ridge of hills about 1,500 feet high between them. It was almost two in the morning when they reached us because it was very tricky for a driver to pick his way through soft dry sugary ground, covered with scrub before entering the mud flat. As soon as the car and trailer arrived, a bell tent was thrown out and we put it up and settled down to a proper night's sleep. On these expeditions we never troubled with guards because our party then of six mechanics for servicing of the aircraft and two car drivers had to forget about guards as we had enough to do.

RECEIVING TWO PRISONERS

George continues:

We woke up at about four thirty, stripped the aircraft and put the fuselage and wings securely on the trailer by about 7 o' clock. We then decided to settle down to the good breakfast of bacon, bread and tea which our driver, Hewitt, had brought along. We sat on the sandy ground enjoying our bacon sandwiches and a nice cup of tea. As the sun rose so did the temperature to about seventy-five degrees when we saw two Arabs and two Turks approaching. When they joined us the Arabs told us that they had been stalking the Turks during the night and took them prisoner. The Arabs produced two hand grenades that they had taken off them.

The two Turks looked very well fed and dressed in lightweight uniforms of wool. They looked like brothers, in fact they looked like twins with rather handsome features and pale complexions.

Makins said, 'I believe these two set out to give us a nice hand grenade awakening only for their captors having come across them.' We shared our breakfast with them and the car returned with a bigger load than we expected! That extra load may have caused the breakdown we had on our way back in Rhum when the Crossley gearbox broke down and held us up for two days until a spare was sent up to replace the damaged one. The prisoners were handed over but we never knew how they got on for they were lucky to have been handed over to us.

RETURN TO RHUM

George continues:

Fortunately we had a spare engine so the machine was back in service within two days. I then went in a Crossley with Lieutenant Siddons, a driver and two other mechanics on a return journey to Rhum with supplies of aviation spirit and a tent to select a suitable ground for the future use of our two Crossleys. We had to go where no cars had never been before!

That journey to Rhum took us about one and a half days to complete because Crossleys often sank up to their axles in sandy ground. We coped by clearing the sand from under the wheels, an easy matter with our hands, and putting a small plank under the wheels along with torn up scrub to give the wheels bite.

Once on the Decie Mudflats where we could speed up to about 35 miles per hour we selected our landing spot where we mechanics stayed put for a couple of weeks.

Our machines arrived from Aquaba after bombing. They flew to us for refuelling and bombing up to carry out more raids at shorter distances from the enemy positions. Meanwhile Arabs attacked the railway between Maan and Mudowwara and further North where the Arabs were making sorties in blowing up trains supported with the armoured cars. The bombing aircraft had kept the Turks penned in at their small fortified positions leaving it so much easier for the wandering bands of Arabs to attack weaker positions. In the absence of enemy opposition in the air our aircraft played havoc until a few months later. They seem to have been shy of flying too far inland over our positions for it would have been disastrous for their pilots who might have been forced down into the hands of the Arabs.

ANOTHER LARGE HAMLA ARRIVES AT THE DROME

George again:

Another similar incident similar took place a couple of days later, one afternoon when our machines were operating all day above Maan and Mudowwara. It was just before Buxton's Scottish Camel Corps were about to make the surprise attack on Mudowwara.

Siddons and I were standing, talking and watching the gradual increase in the number of the Arab tribes who had been passing the fringe of our landing ground near the green scrub ground leading large hill facing us. That was the area which is commonly displayed in photographs and films. Arabs had been travelling by all day long, first in ones and twos then in groups of about a dozen or so quite unlike a disciplined army. More and more of the tribes were crossing over our landing strip and Siddons was getting worried about it. He asked me to go over and try to do something about it. I had to use a lot of tact in asking them to keep a little further out.

As I understood it we were in a very difficult position considering some of the tribes arriving were coming in from Southern Arabia, from Abdulla's area and keeping the Turks hemmed in. Some came from Mesopotamia and those were the tribes who had opposed us during the war in that area. I used my hands to try to explain that this was a landing ground for our 'Tiyaras' [Female flying things], aeroplanes. They began to understand but one Arab, walking alone, stopped when I drew his attention to the problem. He just stood facing me with a very angry look on his face and cursing me in Arabic.

He was an arrogant type of Bedouin, one of those who might use his knife as soon as look at you. He continued his cursing as much to say, you are the one who is trespassing. We don't want you here.

He placed his hand on his dagger. I stared him out and in my turn placed my hand near my revolver and continued to stare at him until he turned away, still cursing me. A few yards on, he turned again to have a look but continued on his way.

The group following that Arab numbered about thirty. Once again I made gestures to show that 'Tiyaras' were approaching. They moved off at an angle showing that they had understood. The Arabs coming up from behind them followed their example. Perhaps those Arabs felt more friendly a few days afterwards when our machines, for the first time carried out a night bombing operation (must have been 21st August) during the Arab attacks on Mudowwara which led to its fall.

X FLIGHT REPORT

The X Flight, Royal Air Force: Summary of Operations for the week ending 10 August 1918 was signed by Siddons in Gueira.

> On the 6th Siddons went to bomb the enemy hangars at Ma'an but found they were empty so he bombed a herd of camels there and the redoubts. Tahonie was certainly an advanced landing ground by then.
> On the 7th Lieut. Divers on a B.E. 2E flew Col. Lawrence to EL JAFAR for the latter to attend an important conference, returning after 2 hours.

ATTACK ON MUDWARRA

The report continues:

> On the 8th, the attack on MUDWARRA took place at dawn this morning accordingly Capt. Siddons left on a B.E. 12A to co-operate. On arrival there, the South redoubt was observed to have been captured, also the middle redoubt was being shelled by the Turks from the North redoubt. The signal HLN was put out meaning bomb the North redoubt. This was done; two gun flashes were observed and position machine-gunned. Three quarters of an hour later, Lieut. Makins and Lt. Sefi on B.E. 12s and 2/Lt. Grant on a B.E. 2E arrived; the North redoubt was again bombed and machine-gunned. In all 35- 20lb Coopers bombs and 565 rounds S.A.A. [Small Arms Ammunition] fired. When these machines arrived back at GUEIRA, Lieut. Divers on a B.E. 12A left to reconnoitre the station etc. On arrival, the 3 redoubts and the station were found to be captured, all men and camels being camped between the redoubts and the station. The signal HLII was put out in the station meaning come again to-morrow. The machines then went south, bombing and machine-gunning KALAAT EI AHMAR station and redoubt. Lieut. Junor on a Nieuport went at dawn to the landing ground at TAHONIE, landing there, and returning later in the morning. No E.A. were observed although 2 were reported just before the machine arrived at advanced landing ground

Lawrence mentioned the same attack and the aircraft with:

> Siddons flew me back to Guweira [one] evening, and in the night at Akaba I told Dawnay, just arrived, that life was full, but slipping smoothly. Next morning we heard by aeroplane how Buxton's force had fared at Mudowwara. They decided to assault it before dawn mainly by means of bombers, in three parties, one to enter the station, the other two for the main redoubts.[40]

The report continues:

> On the 9th Lieut. Sefi on a B.E. 2E left with 5- 20lb. Coopers bombs to reconnoitre MUDAWARA and South. The station was still occupied by the

British so machine proceeded South and bombed DHAT EL HAJ. 2/Lt. Oldfield left on a Nieuport to patrol district North of MAAN. One E.A. was sighted and engaged: E.A. tried to ret to MA'AN aerodrome but was headed off to North. 2/Lt. Oldfield followed up E.A. who was going very fast with nose down. Fight was broken off 4 miles North of ANEIZA owing to low altitude and strong enemy action from ground. Machine was afterwards reported by a Bedouin to have crashed South of JURF EL DERWISH.

On the 10th Lt. Makins on a B.E. 2E left to reconnoitre the line South of MUDWARA. Nothing of importance was seen except a party of about 100 strong of infantry in a cutting 3 miles South of KALAAT EL AHMAR. These were bombed and machine-gunned. Lieut. Sefi left on a B.E. 2E to find out position of the cars belonging to the 10 pounder R.F.A. Battery on the MUDWARA road. During the period 27th July to 10th August 10 E.A. have been reported.

GUEIRA. Shelter trenches have now been completed. Carpenters are at present employed on repairing the outer ribs of Nieuport lower planes. A hangar, spares and tents have been transported to the new advanced landing ground at TAHONIE. It is very difficult to get the aerodrome cleared etc. since only labour obtainable comes from the Sheritian Army who are of a very independent nature and only work when it suits them.

Lawrence had this to say about both ground and air attacks.

The northern redoubt, which had a gun, seemed better-hearted and splashed its shot freely into the station yard, and at our troops. Buxton, under cover of the southern redoubt, directed the fire of Brodie's guns which, with their usual deliberate accuracy, sent in shell after shell. Siddons came over in his machines and bombed it, while the Camel Corps from north and east and west subjected the breastworks to severe Lewis gun-fire. At seven in the morning the last of the enemy surrendered quietly. We had lost four killed and ten wounded. The Turks lost twenty-one killed, and one hundred and fifty prisoners, with two field-guns and three machine-guns.[41]

BRITISH AND TURKISH BATTLE CASUALTIES ARRIVE

George recalls his experiences of post-battle casualties.

Buxton had carried out a night attack, just before dawn. It resulted in a sharp short and stiff fight. Some of his wounded were brought to our hangars leaving behind a sergeant killed in action along with a small number other ranks. Among the wounded who were brought to us were a captain and a few privates. The captain with a body wound was a stretcher case and so was a corporal who had a severe wound in the lower part of his abdomen. They tried to look cheerful but the corporal [who] was in a very bad condition described some incidents in the fight.

The fight was tough. He praised the Turks for their fighting qualities and stressed the spirit of one young Turk age about eighteen. He fought like hell with his bayonet until one of our lads threw a Mills bomb at him. That was a pity but he had to be stopped. He really deserved a medal, not a hand grenade, for his bayonet work. A medical orderly told me the corporal was in a very bad way with a wound that may have proved fatal on in his journey to Egypt. There was no travelling medical unit with the Arabs.

We made the few Turkish wounded as comfortable as possible in our hangars. Some sat on the sandy floor, others leaned on our tool boxes to give them the ease but all the while their pain and suffering needed medical attention which we could not give them. The only consolation we could give was friendly smiles and cigarettes. We have a certain amount of respect to our enemies after a battle for we realise they too are also human. The Turks did have some respect for us but they have a job to do, just as we did.

It does make me wonder why men should be forced to kill on behalf of a powerful few and why now, our children should live to fight all over again. Is man mad and fighting a relief for his distorted mind?

I know it is selfish greed and lust because man is never satisfied.

Did Lawrence show up hypocrisy and did he show us all the true meaning of Christian teaching. And I am positive he behaved like a true Christian who would not be enticed into politics and lived a closed social life.

X FLIGHT REPORT

The X Flight, Royal Air Force, Summary of Operations for the week ending 17 August 1918 was signed by Siddons in Gueira.

Under 'AKABA' he wrote:

On the morning of the 14th inst the Workshop caught fire and was put out with some difficulty, but not much damage.

In the evening the Workshop Leyland Lorry was completely burnt.

Siddons' matter-of-fact statement was, however, graphically described by George.

In August, after a very busy day of operations, all machines had been made serviceable and ready for morning. All NCOs had been very busy right up to seven thirty when we retired to our tents to wash off the oil and dirt that had accumulated mixed with the sweat that trickled off us.

We were about to get our billycans and collect our evening meal of stew, when our hopes were suddenly dashed by the report of an explosion.

We all ran out, amazed to see our Leyland workshop lorry in flames. Immediately all hands were frantically busy to trying to prevent its total loss by throwing the fine soft dry sands of the Wadi Araba over the burning vehicle. Some Egyptian soldiers, who had then recently joined us to do guard duties at night, had about three spades which they used to shovel up and throw the sand. Although we went all-out to save the lorry, it was useless to quell the flames. We just had to stand by until it collapsed in a total wreck.

The next morning, Captain Siddons, tried to compile his report in consultation with the senior base NCO responsible for camp personnel. They had not discovered the cause of the fire so I was approached by Siddons later in the morning when working on our aircraft.

'Sergeant Hynes I want you to examine the debris and see if you can find the cause of the fire.'

'I'll do that now!'

Captain Siddons walked away leaving me with the mechanic who was on duty to look after the electric generating units.

I had a good look round of the engine debris knowing that the Leyland had hardly been used since it arrived back in November 1917, brought in from the Gulf beach foot by foot to get it up to our camp. Only the steel chassis and wheels survived the fire. Even the solid rubber tyres were burnt to carbon.

In my search of the debris, I found the screw top cap of the petrol tank that contained the fuel for the four-cylinder engine unit with the electric generator. I picked it up and showed it to the mechanic who was very worried and upset at the loss and as anyone would be when in his charge during duty.

'I can see what caused by the fire. You had taken the top off to refill the tanks when it was running, the generator spilt some of the petrol, it ran down on the generator and was ignited. Particles of sand had got under the carbon brushes resulting in sparking which ignited the petrol which in turn ignited the fuel in the tanks.'

The mechanic replied. 'That's correct sergeant!'

I screwed the cap on the top of a burst tank and turned to the mechanic. 'Don't you worry about this because I will report, "The petrol pipe sprung a leak, petrol had run down on to the generator and set the fuel alight also the electric dynamo. The petrol tank placed over the dynamo should be removed from there and fitted to a safe position to avoid such accidents in the future." That's my report that clears you from blame!'

I felt that the mechanic was not to blame as he hadn't really done much on motors and was ignorant about generating units. It would have been an injustice if he had been found guilty of negligence on duty. His chances of promotion would have been shattered.

The mechanics, like all tradesmen, were graded. This airman was an expert in his own class of work performing essential duties to keep in support of our aircraft. He was our official and one and only photographer and was therefore responsible for processing and enlarging the pictures taken over enemy positions.

He was the straight honest type of man and I felt it was my duty not to have his name placed on report to Cairo because their first reaction was usually, 'Somebody I expect has been smoking.' The vehicle was destroyed but it was after all wartime. I realised that vehicles can be replaced but not men. That man could well have been killed in the explosion. I had told a white lie to save the man from shame.

Makins referred to the clearing up after the fire in his report.

X FLIGHT REPORT

The X Flight, Royal Air Force, Report for the week ending 25 August 1918 was signed by Lieut. Makins for Capt. Commanding X Flight in Gueira.

> AKABA – M.T. Work has been carried on clearing up all the debris of the fire in the Workshop and lorry. There is a landing ground at EL JAFAR.
>
> 19th August. The machine attacked by Lt. Oldfield and the 9th inst has now been found to have landed just S. of JURDUN station. It was so badly damaged that had to be dismantled and was taken to KATRANI.
>
> 19th. A machine was flown to the landing ground at EL JAFAR to arrange about bombs etc. for night bombing, but returned same day, the stores not having arrived.
>
> 20th (August) Lt. Junor took a B.E. 12 up after dark to see if night bombing operations were possible from GUEIRA. Everything was found O.K. so it was decided that it should be carried out from that place.

On the 21st night bombing began. This may have been a good tactical move though a hazardous one. The enemy had learned to hide targets during the early daylight hours when they knew the British machines carried out their attacks. During the hotter times of the day they could carry on with their activities knowing that the X Flight aircraft would not be flying over on aggressive raids.

In this report he says that 'the personnel of TAHONIE was evacuated together with spares etc.' the hangar being left there for possible future use. The question remains – did this become place X?

George wrote:

> Back in Gueira, our hangar had been finished and some additional men and machines had been sent to us from our base back at Aquaba and we were joined by Captain Siddons in preparation for our advance. They had been members of General Murray's army but some had been posted from Egypt. Some were skilled tradesmen who had been transferred from other units into the RFC. Two more machines flew in from Egypt, a BE12 and the Martinsyde Scout. This meant we spent longer periods at Mudowwara carrying out top overhauls to keep our machines serviceable. Those overhauls reduced the needs for complete overhauls as we used teams of four in a marquee at Aquaba. We kept a spare RAF engine to make a quick replacement when needed.

INTENSIVE OPERATIONS

George writes:

> Our operations continued from dawn to dusk and for the first time we commenced night flying after receiving a portable searchlight from Egypt. It could be carried by two men using poles. I examined and tested it for use on the field.
>
> After increased bombings of Mudowwara, before its fall, I was obliged to travel by air with Captain Junor. During that flight I saw the largest camel convoy ever moving up towards Gueira as they slowly moved forward in a single column.
>
> I returned the next day and our night flying began. Junor was the first night flyer to take off with a load of 20 pound bombs. I was told to have the portable searchlight light carried out on to the landing ground and to switch on the beam when we received a Verey light signal as agreed by Siddons and Junor.
>
> It was a very dark night and so our pilot had to gain a suitable height in order to fly over the hills just ahead of our ground. We were all set for Junor's return and anxious that he should be successful and make a safe return as he had had no night flying experience in Arabia. He was however, a fearless pilot only content when in the air.
>
> After he had been away for about one and a half hours we heard the drone of his machine and started up the generator ready for that signal as no lights were showing on the drome.
>
> As Junor approached Captain Siddons and I stood close to the searchlight. Two Verey lights were fired so I switched on the beam aiming it low over the landing ground to give him a long run for safety's sake. The aircraft glided in over our heads and into the beam of light making a perfect landing and Junor jumped out reporting that all had been successful. He and Siddons moved off to their tent.
>
> Further flights were made as our machines opened up from dawn to dusk, with a few more night raids on the eve of Buxton's attack on Mudowwara.
>
> After the fall of Mudowwara, wounded prisoners and our few wounded had to be taken to Aquaba on tenders. A battle prize, a small brass cannon, about 300 pounds in weight which fired a shell of two inches diameter, was brought into our camp. This weapon stood about four feet high having a maximum angle of aim about 15 degrees. Damaging at short range it had been used in battle at Mudowwara. It looked comical to me, more like an obsolete antique. It did not look suitable for use against racing camels in surprise attacks.

George recalls:

> I was told to return to Aquaba. Among the personnel who had remained there during the attacks were a few mechanics, about six. All were men who had only been training, carrying out 'top overhauls' of a stripped down RAF engine. They had to learn from the manuals because among them were a stores clerk, an orderly room clerk, an electrician and a photographer. A new arrival, a second Lieutenant was in charge.

SEPTEMBER 1918

X Flight Report

The X Flight, Royal Air Force, Report for the week ending 7 September 1918 was signed by Lt Makins in Gueira.

> 1st. There was no Flying this day. [He no doubt wrote that because flying was virtually a daily duty! But he did report more attacks on the enemy at Maan later in the week.]
> Flying missions were becoming fewer. Lt. OLDFIELD flying over EL HESA Station noticed a large fortified camp of the enemy made up of 45 bell tents and shelters. A train load of troops in open trucks was seen. They were machine gunned.

X Flight Report

The X Flight Report for the week ending 14 September 1918 was signed by Siddons in Gueira.

> Arrived at Jafar. Had trouble with OWD ABU TIE, who had been refused a lift by a car full of Armenians and Drus.

More interesting attacks. Turkish Concentration Camp? What then is a concentration camp as used here?

The mysterious place X showed up again here, in this report.

> 12th Lt. Junor reported on a B.E. 2E from 'X' where he is on temporary duty: making the following report 3-9-18. Lt. Junor left GUEIRA with 2 Crossley tenders and 5 O.R. 1 load of petrol left at Negb Post and the 1 tender sent back to GUEIRA.

Was Gueira then being called X? Or was it Negb Post?

The report continues:

13th. Lt. Junor left on B.E. 12a with tender spares and supplies for 'X'. The B.E. 2E left for 'X' but was unable to climb and crashed outside the Aerodrome. The engine was taken out and sent to AKABA arriving there at 1515. It was immediately put in a B.E. 2E at AKABA and the machine was then flown to GUEIRA arriving there at 1800.

Place X could have been located on some very high ground which the B.E.2E was unable to reach.

It could have been about this time that George wrote about here.

Captain Siddons said to me, 'Hynes, I want you to go down to take charge of servicing from there. You have been recommended for promotion to Flight Sergeant.' Personally, I would have preferred to have been in on the advanced finish. Although the benefits of my new posting would have been a change from the hardships we had to put up with near the front.

AN AIR RAID ON AKABA

George again:

I was only two days at Aquaba when a Crossley came down from Gueira to take us back. Siddons had been opposed by an enemy machine but his gun had jammed so I went by tender towards the Wadi Ithm. My attention was drawn to a volley from a HMS *Humber* and looking up we spotted a German machine about 6,000 ft high, flying in the direction of the village. It was the first time I had set eyes on the battery of French seventy-fives who fired four shells from an escarpment close to the hills bordering Aquaba running the whole length of Wadi Araba up to the Wadi Ithm.

The aircraft dropped its last few bombs into a belt of palm trees that sheltered the village from the Gulf beach. I heard later that a couple of Arabs had been killed and a few injured. Apparently, the enemy aircraft had dropped about three bombs in an attempt to hit the *Humber* but overshot that target. Some of the bombs that missed dropped in the Gulf and did bring up a quantity of dead fish for the Arabs in Aquaba and I feel certain that brought a new technique to Aquaba in getting supplies of fresh fish ever afterwards.

After arriving back at Gueira, I heard that Captain Siddons was annoyed with the mechanics. Previously I had kept a check on the Lewis's synchronised gun gear to prevent stoppages but the job had been placed in the hands of inexperienced, conscripted mechanics. I tested the gun with a few rounds and discovered a mechanical defect; a feed pawl spring which had lost much of its tension. That was replaced and passed as OK.

The next morning, I returned to Aquaba but fell into further trouble

Before the staff moved up to Gueira, a stone building was built, about 30 ft long and 15ft wide with a height of about 12 ft. It was to be used as a workshop. It looked as if Cairo was planning a longer war although Lawrence had said, in March four months previously, that we must finish the war in the next few months.

A FIRE IN THE NEW STONE WORKSHOP

George continues:

I called on the personnel in order to be acquainted with their duties. There I was met with moans and groans from mechanics engaged on the engine overhauls. They complained that they never received promotion as first class mechanics, a promotion which would have increased their pay from two shillings per day to four shillings plus their sixpence a day extra allowances granted as Hejaz pay for special duty.

That was actually a matter they should have discussed with their own NCO in charge and with their commanding officer. By all accounts this resentment had been simmering for some time like the mood they were in when they refused to be inoculated on arrival in October 1917. I had been left with only one good mechanic, Air Mechanic Gaunt, so I did what I could to appease them and reported the matter.

I then went into the stone workshop where I he got caught up washing out the oil channels of the engine crankshaft resting on a bright new tin rectangular container. While I was chatting there with a mechanic about the job, there was a sudden great flashover as petrol ignited in a tank. Without fire extinguishers, no fire sheets to smother the flames or to damp it down, we just had to let the fire burn out. The only thing in the workshop was that container and a couple of lights which the electrician fitted up while standing on a step ladder.

The matter was reported to the officer in charge but we had to get away quickly to receive a visiting machine which had landed, a Bristol fighter, piloted by Lieutenant Murphy of the No. 1 Australian Squadron from Gaza.

We received the machine and taxied it over. The pilots and gunner reported and I was called into the Orderly Room tent, where we were charged with neglect of duty. The new equipment officer i/c on Araba base stores, decided that somebody must have been smoking and caused the fire at the time. He called upon Lt. Murphy to sit as a witness. I made my report saying that there was no person smoking and the cause of the fire was very easily explained. The temperature was about one hundred and ten degrees that afternoon and the sun's rays had been glaring on all sides of the bright new tin container concentrating and intensifying the sun's rays. The resultant high temperature ignited the petrol vapour in the tank and it burst into flames. The container had been received a week previously and had then been used in a shaded marquee.

Nobody was smoking. In fact I had no cigarettes, I doubt if anyone did at time. Gaunt was not smoking nor the electrician. Still, the admin officer's report was forwarded to Captain Siddons with a copy sent on to headquarters in Cairo and as far as I am concerned I am still on a charge!

I do know that a similar incident occurred at Heliopolis when the squadron received a large supply of aviation spirit, high-octane pure fuel without additives. It arrived in four-gallon tins and when exposed to open sunlight a tin had exploded. The result was that about 500 tins went up in flames.

Further proof lies in the fact that we never received many matches at a time when few rations ever came through to us. We often used pieces of glass to light fires or cigarettes. In fact if we had ever had such luxuries as eggs, we could have cooked them without a fire. The young admin officer may well have been surprised that Captain Siddons never followed up that charge.

Sergeant Ross who had been orderly room clerk once told me that afterwards a very strong letter was sent out from headquarters protesting about my being placed on that charge. When I returned to Egypt after our operations, and Colonel Grant Dalton had flown over commending me on my service in Arabia, he told me, 'You are classified as the engine expert of the Middle East.' He then offered me another position with promotion to take over as senior NCO at Shaluffa in Egypt.

I was later recalled to Gueira to operate from there for a while just shortly before the final assault on the Turks. An advance party of two Crossleys had gone ahead to Azrak with two machines. Corporal Wheeler was one of the two mechanics flown in to meet Lawrence. Captain Junor was escorted by Lieutenant Murphy in his Bristol fighter. Murphy and his air gunner had been loaned to us from Palestine to cover our slower machine, the BE12 use by Lieutenant Junor at Azrak.

I arrived back at Gueira and I was told to have a rest for a change for I had been on duty each day since I had been at Aquaba in charge of the advanced operations ground crews and everything applicable to all for the supervision including stocks of fuel on our positions so that we were well supplied to meet our requirements in air duties according to circumstances. I was allowed to lie in until eight o' clock!

When I got back to duty after my breakfast hour I was asked how I enjoyed my lie-in as they were surprised that I had not heard Murphy in his fighter roaring past my tent missing it by inches. The three-fifty horsepower Rolls Royce was a very noisy plane and so that was why they were surprised that I had slept on.

I was also surprised to hear that the two machines the Bristol and the BE12 with Junor piloting it had set off for Azrak [about 200 miles north north east of Gueira] where they had landed for the operation with Lawrence and as I had had air duties both in the Palestine and the Arabia. It would have been a joy to have been allowed to go on that journey.

An article on Capt. Ross Smith of the Australian Flying Corps had this to say:

> In August of 1918, Fiesal's Army was based at Azrak outside of Deraa, where the remainder of the German Fleiger Abteilungs were based. Lawrence had received some clapped out old BE12s as X Flight to support his operations. The BEs didn't last long. A Bristol Fighter from 1 Squadron was sent to replace the lost BE12s however that aircraft got caught in a combat with nine German aircraft and had its rear longerons shot through. Lieutenant 'Spud' Murphy and Lieutenant Fred Hawley managed to fix the aircraft and fly it back to the Australian aerodrome.
>
> The Bristol was replaced with three Bristols, with the aircrews of, Captain Ross 'Hadji' Smith and Lieutenant Pard Mustard, Lieutenant Eustice 'Useless' Headlam and Lieutenant William Lilly, and Captain George Peters and Lieutenant James Trail.[42]

SEPTEMBER 1918

AUSTRALIAN PILOT SHOOTS DOWN ENEMY PLANE

George heard of a particular dog fight.

> A very interesting story came to us of the last fight in the air when a German/Turkish pilot decided to have a ding-dong fight with Lieutenant Murphy the Australian in the Bristol. Both machines engaged in close combat using every move that could be carried out twisting, diving, looping until one of them had to perish and finally Murphy had won through with the enemy machine falling in pieces with wings falling away and in flames but Murphy's machine had been very badly shot up also. The rumour was that the enemy pilot was an Austrian Prince and a great fighter.
>
> Lieutenant Murphy and his gunner, sent down from Palestine in the Bristol fighter, had landed two weeks before the final push by Lawrence and the Arab army at Aquaba. He went on to Gueira until the advance began.

ALLENBY'S BIG OFFENSIVE

The Manchesters were in action again, this time successfully taking part in the last major offensive there at Megiddo, on 19 September 1918.

Within three hours the Turkish lines, held by the Turkish Eighth Army, had been broken. Open warfare was the order of the day, in complete contradiction to what had, and was, occurring in other theatres. During the Megiddo offensive, the cavalry advanced over 70 miles in just thirty-six hours, performing what was an early form of *blitzkrieg*. It was a total defeat for the Turkish Forces.

George recounts:

> News came to us about the horrible atrocities that had been committed on Sheikh Tallal's villagers. Some bayonets used on the women had been left in

bodies. Sights that would make any man mad with a rage. Tallal avenged himself by carrying out similar atrocities but none matched the slaughter of a whole village.

An order given by Auda and his brother Sheikhs was that the Arabs were not restrained from avenging Tallal and his people. A golden sovereign was offered for each dead Turk.

Allenby's final offensive began when the Arab force was about 20 miles south-east of Deraa. Lawrence left from there in a Bristol to Allenby's HQ then joined with the Arabs for the attack on Damascus. Recce by X Flight from Gueira confirmed evacuation of Ma'an on the 22nd X had to pack up and leave.

On 21 September 1918 RAF aircraft in Palestine attacked and destroyed the retreating Turkish Seventh Army at Wadi el Fara. Lawrence, ever grateful for air support, wrote:

> It was the RAF which converted the retreat into a rout, which had abolished their telephone and telegraph connections, had blocked their lorry columns and scattered their infantry units. (Royal Air Force History)

X FLIGHT REPORT

The X Flight, Royal Air Force, Report for the week ending 21 September 1918 although signed by Capt. V.D. Siddons in Gueira was written by Lt Latham standing in for the CO.

> 18th. Lts Murphy and Hawley on Bristol Fighter left to locate Arab forces and reco line 12 miles N. DERAA. They carried out a reco of BOSRA ESKI SHAM but could not approach DERAA owing to pressure from 9 Enemy Scouts, & could not definitely locate Arab Army.

This document included a report from 'X' from Lt Junor. (This 'coy' reference to X occurred a few times during the last months of 1918. It must have referred to a particular advanced landing ground – Tahonie or Gueira perhaps!)

> 15th. [September] Lts. Murphy and Hawley on Bristol Fighter left to reco line to 12 miles N. DERRA. On returning they met E.A. two seater and after long fight the E.A. was seen to stall then fall and crash in flames about 10 miles N.E. MAFRAK. Lt. Hawley dropped message on Armoured Cars reporting all clear to MEZERIB and also that his machine was badly damaged and unable to fly the following day.
>
> Signed by F. Latham, Lieut. R.A.F. COMMANDING 'X' FLIGHT. Royal Air Force.

This may have been the incident mentioned on page 18 of the book *Winged Promises* where it says that on 15 September 1918, X Flight's Bristol shot down an enemy two-seater but itself sustained heavy damage.

In a subsection, of the report dated 21 September 1918, headed, 'REPORT FROM "X" FROM LT. DIVERS' was written:

17th [September] Lt. Junor on B.E.12a left to land by H.A.C.B. near the line. Lts. Murphy and Hawley on Bristol Fighter landed, having flown via DERAA from Palestine bearing dispatches for Col Joyce. They report having engaged 6 Hun Scouts N.E. of DERAA which were forced to land on DERAA aerodrome. The B.E.12a was observed overturned on the ground about 6 miles N. of DERAA and close to H.A.C.B. and H.Q. cars.

These two intrepid pilots, who undertook courageous exploits in the service of X Flight, got themselves into some administrative trouble with Headquarters Royal Air Force Middle East for allegedly not reporting in to an orderly officer in Suez after a flight from Aboukir in early June 1918.

George had great respect and admiration for Junor whose standing was very high among everyone including the great Lawrence himself as one particular incident reveals.

Several sources including *Winged Promises* mention that after six D.H.9s of No. 14 Squadron bombed Deraa on 16 and 17 September 1918, eight German aeroplanes were sent to Jenin, 50 miles to the west. There they attacked an Arab force trying to blow up a stretch of railway line. A solitary British machine appeared, a BE.12 piloted by Captain Junor.

Lawrence described Junor's courageous attack upon eight German aircraft thus:

We watched with mixed feelings, for this hopelessly old-fashioned machine made him cold meat for any one of the enemy scouts or two-seaters: but at first he astonished them as he rattled in with his two guns. They scattered for a careful look at this unexpected opponent. He flew westward across the line and they went after in pursuit, with that amiable weakness of aircraft for a hostile machine, however important the ground target. We were left in perfect peace.[43]

Junor landed when he had run out of fuel. His machine was damaged on landing but he managed to scramble clear before it was destroyed by a well-placed bomb dropped by a pursuer. Junor immediately got into a Ford car, which was then driven along the railway towards Deraa where he blew up some track.

In his modest memoirs, George made an appropriate comment.

The Martinsyde Scouts had a fuel capacity for three hundred miles range and any one of them would have given Junor a fighting chance. The BE12 never had the speed to face the Fokker or the Taube. Junor had done well to escape death in that last operation and deserved his battle award.

He added:

Junor was a devil for anything. That probably dates back to his infantry training. He was in his element when he went in the armoured cars with his

Lewis gun. That was when the remainder of our aircraft were left at Gueira. Captain Junor had taken on a job no doubt following orders but he had very little chance to be successful in downing the enemy in combat both in manoeuvrability in dogfights and no rear gunner to protect him from attack on the blind tail end of his machine. He must be given great credit for taking up an aircraft which was totally unsuitable for combat; but he was a keen fighter who feared nobody, either in the air or on the ground. Each of the four good Martinsyde Scouts had a fuel capacity of three hundred miles range. Any one of them would have given Junor a fighting chance supported by the other three. That flimsy BE12 did not have the speed to face up to the Fokker or Taube. The BE type of aircraft would not have been sent out over the enemy lines during our Arabian operations without at least two Martinsydes with them because they were bombers and fighters, fifteen miles per hour faster.

In his turn, the reporter, Lowell Thomas described the same episode.

Until Lawrence's one surviving machine, an antiquated old bus piloted by Captain Junor, came trundling up from Azarak and sailed square into the middle of the whole German squadron, Lawrence and his followers watched this with mixed feelings, for each of the four enemy two seaters and four scout planes was more than the equal of one prehistoric British machine. With both skill and good luck Captain Junor cruised right through the German birdmen and led the whole circus off to the westward. Twenty minutes later the plucky Junor came tearing back through the air with his attendant swarm of enemy planes and signalled down to Lawrence that he had run out of petrol. He landed within fifty yards of the Arab column, and his BE flopped over on its back. A German Halberstadt dived on it at once and scored a direct hit with a bomb that blew the little British machine to bits. Fortunately, Junor had jumped out of the seat a moment before. The only part of his BE that wasn't destroyed was the Lewis machine gun. Within half an hour the plucky pilot had transferred it to a Ford truck and was tearing around outside Deraa, raking the Turks with his tracer bullets.[44]

In his account, George added this:

The BE12 was a suicide machine which could have coped in flights over Turkish lines into a hornets' nest of the enemy aircraft had it been escorted by Lieutenant Murphy in his Bristol fighter. Even then he would have had a bad time if two or more machines attacked them.

AUSTRALIAN AIR FORCE ENCOUNTER

Meanwhile, according to an article on the Australian Air Force another Flight was busy.

On the 22nd of September Ross Smith along with the other Australians were having breakfast at Azrak in Fiesel's camp, when a warning came across for a German bombing raid. Smith and Mustard with Headlam and Lilly took off and caught the DFW along with the two Pfalz Scouts.

[Benz engines powering the DFW series of aircraft made them formidable foes. These aircraft were made mostly of wood and fabric with some metal used in the tail section. The pilot used a single 7.92-mm Spandau type MG08/15 synchronised machine gun in the fixed-forward position whereas the observer used his single machine gun in the rear.

The Pfalz D.III was produced in large numbers, first for the Bavarian forces but later for the Imperial German air force. It was an agile fighter best used in high-speed diving attacks on Allied reconnaissance balloons and aircraft. It was armed with two 7.92-mm machine guns.]

The Bristols caught the DFW and their fire set it alight, the DFW crashing near Mafrak The Pfalz Scouts then broke for the aerodrome at Deraa, the Bristols were unable to catch them but did strafe them on the ground after they had landed.

The Bristols returned to Azrak and the aircrews continued their breakfast as the *Blackwood's Magazine* recounts.

While L. [Lawrence] and the airmen were having breakfast with us, a Turkish plane was observed, making straight for us. One of the airmen... hurried off to down the intruder. This he successfully did, and the Turkish plane fell in flames near the railway. He then returned and finished his porridge, which had been kept hot for him meanwhile! But not for him a peaceful breakfast that morning. He had barely reached the marmalade stage when another Turkish plane appeared. Up hurried the Australian again; but this Turk was too wily and scuttled back to Deraa, only to be chased by R [Peters] on another machine, which sent him down in flames.

The article continues:

The paraphrased story isn't quite accurate, however after the Bristols returned at 10.30 am another warning was raised this time for three Pfalz aircraft approaching. Ross Smith and Pard Mustard rose to greet them, and in the ensuing engagement drove down all three aircraft, two landing nearby the railway and running along the ground to Turkish outposts. The third made for Deraa, landing there. Smith and Mustard chased the third aircraft before returning to the two downed aircraft, strafing them until they were unfit to fly.[45]

In September 1918 Arab allies moved into Qasr el Azraq, 60 miles from Amman and two of X Flight's aircraft joined them there to keep an eye on Deraa, 70 miles to the north-west. T.E.L. was cutting railway lines around there. Amman has a prominent place in the Old Testament. It stood close to the Ammonite fortress of Rabah. Joab, King David's captain, besieged that town and its fortress. It was to there that Uriah the Hittite was sent to his death so that David could marry his widow. Ezekiel wanted to turn the town into a stable for camels and Amos thought it was not a place fit for human habitation!

After the War Amman stayed on as an RAF aerodrome, home for Ninak planes, the de Havilland DH9, a bomber which formed the backbone of the Royal Air Force's post-war colonial force.

SUMMARY OF LT JUNOR'S REPORT

Siddons' report was characteristically terse. The X Flight Report for the week ending 28 September 1918, signed by him, with characteristic British understatement, recorded a 'brush' with the enemy in September, 1918.

A subsection of that report was headed 'SUMMARY OF LT JUNOR'S REPORT'.

19-9-18 Hangar was taken down and the cover used as a bivouac.

20-9-18 Dump was moved to the English Camp. Lt Junor arrived at 'X' on an armoured car having burnt his machine 6 miles W of DERAA, it having been shot down by 3 Enemy machines and then bombed. He reports having saved his Guns and instruments and magnetos, and then attached himself temporarily to the Hedjaz Armoured Car battery.

21-9-18 Lt. Junor prepared to leave for GUEIRA, only awaiting the escort of an armoured car. A pilot on a B.F. [Bristol Fighter] from PALESTINE landed, with dispatches, and returned to RAMLEH taking Lt Col Lawrence with him, his own observer remaining at 'X'.

22-9-18 B.F. returned from RAMLEH with Lt Col Lawrence and returned later to UMTAIYE....

X FLIGHT REPORT

The X Flight, Royal Air Force: Summary of Operations for the week ending 28 September 1918 was signed by Siddons in Akaba.

X Flight pilots continued aggressive actions: bombing JURDUN and trains despite heavy anti-aircraft fire; 23rd Latham bombed troops leaving Ma'an; Oldfield bombed a train; 24th Sefi and Grant bombed enemy troops; Murphy and Hawley machine gunned troop train; on 25th Oldfield went in search of a party on temporary duty from 'X'. He landed at JAFAR DEPRESSION where the cars were and returned with AM/2 Yarham to GUEIRA. 26th.

Junor and Divers brought back a Crossley tender with an O.R. on temporary duty at X.

The very last aggressive action taken by X Flight was on 25 September, 1918. Siddons then reported that Lts Murphy and Hawley on a B.F. (Bristol Fighter or Brisfit or Biff) 'left to watch enemy movement to N. Nothing of importance was observed N to HESA but train at HESA was machine gunned.'

The SUMMARY OF LT JUNOR'S REPORT mentioned the dismantling of a hangar for use as a bivouac; a dump moved to the English Camp; Junor arriving in an armoured car after his having burnt his machine and salved the guns, instruments and magnetos; his joining in the fighting in the armoured car section. On the 21st a pilot from Palestine landed with dispatches and took Lawrence back with him while his observer stayed at 'X'. On the 22nd Lawrence returned from Ramleh.

Despite all that flying action by X Flight, on the 26th the whole Flight was ordered to begin a complete evacuation from Gueira. According to an X Flight Report for the week ending 28 September 1918 it used five tenders and a little later another seven tenders with trailers; three pilots also left. The Nieuport was dismantled and packed for shipment. Eighteen camels left for Akaba with stores and spares. The evacuation continued all week but strangely a Lt Bankes-Jones brought in a B.E.12 for X Flight where it was tested by Divers before its return to Suez.

On the same day, 1 October, that Lawrence and the Arabs took Damascus, X Flight was given permission to dump stores on the quay at Akaba ready for shipment and a wire road was laid from the camp to the quay. Vehicles and twenty-five camels were used in the move.

X FLIGHT REPORT

The X Flight Report for the week ending 5 October 1918, signed by Siddons in Akaba, confirmed the complete evacuation of Gueira. X Squadron left for Suez.

George wrote:

> There is no doubt that the secret planning by Allenby and Lawrence along with the sudden defeat of the Turks had surprised both Whitehall and the military staff in Cairo. It certainly surprised our detachment based in Gueira where machines were expected to be used in more prolonged operations. The speed of the attack by Lawrence and Feisal's army was a really big surprise for everyone. All credit should be given to the preparations made by Lawrence, Auda, Nazir, Ali and Jaffa Pasha and all their tribal sheikhs who were all able to make one united effort. The whole Turkish administration in the field was unable to stand up to it. We were given immediate orders to get back to Aquaba as soon as possible; never once did we expect to be in Suez before the end of October 1918, but we were!

LAWRENCE IN AKABA TAKES US OUT FOR THE DAY

George remembered a day out to a fascinating island with Lawrence as their guide.

Lawrence had arrived at Aquaba about two days after he left Allenby in that first meeting with Feisal in Damascus. I was surprised to see him arrive to join our small party about to go on an afternoon's outing. The commander of HMS *Humber* arranged for a naval pinnace to take us down the Gulf to an island that lay with a lovely lagoon which Lawrence had a visited before the war during his archaeological surveys. Newcombe and he had visited the place just before the war.

Lawrence did not wear his white satin cloak and golden dagger as his critic Aldington suggested as an actor's ornament but he did wear his head-dress. We all did on that that day out. He showed no sign of strain from those last days of fighting. He was calm and as boyish looking as ever smiling with the pleasure of our company. There was nothing of the conquering hero about him and no signs of self-importance that was often displayed by the professional soldier.

In fact he was going to show us a small island in a beautiful setting undisturbed by man for centuries. He told us how Solomon had built his ships on the bed of a dry lake which at one time was filled by waters from the Gulf at high tides when the ships could then be launched into the lovely clear lagoon.

As we entered the basin-like lagoon, we peered down into the bottom where we could clearly see large sponges, clean sand, sea anemones and many species of fish. There were no sharks as it was enclosed by a white coral reef which circled the island. We waded ankle deep through its waters to stand on dry land. Lawrence was our guide as we stepped on to the island.

Standing within the fifty foot walls of the lagoon was like being in a huge bowl of sand hills that had protected it from sand storms for centuries. It was a beautiful place.

It was an undisturbed work of nature never put to use by Arabs or Egyptians although situated on the Sinai coast only a short distance from Aquaba. The island in the centre of the lagoon was about one hundred and fifty yards long and about seventy yards across with [a] fairly flat surface covered with small pieces of assorted rocks and thin layers of mica set in the marble stone. I brought a piece back with me.

The island was more than about five feet above water level but an entrance had been made about 30 ft wide. Running parallel with the lake on the side nearest the entrance was a low wall of coral loosely built and about three feet high. We listened in silence to Lawrence as he explained its purpose during Solomon's time.

The island was besieged during Solomon's period when he was compelled to build his ships and store food, mainly fish caught in the lagoon, and so the dried lake was where Solomon built his ships. When a ship was completed, the low built wall was removed to enable the ship to be launched.

On the island there were three six feet deep pits about four feet in diameter containing large flat fish as one might now see on our own market stalls selling salt fish. We took one fish out. It smelt clean and well preserved.

Because of the length of time it had lain in the pit, it could not be cut with a knife. The fish was as hard as steel, so Sergeant Clemence of the Royal Engineers, one of our group during this outing, obtained a hacksaw from the naval pinnace. We used it to cut the fish into pieces for each of us to take way as souvenirs. The salted fish seem to be as good as our modern product of today.

We spent about an hour on the island of Huarin which we then called Solomon's island and returned to the jetty at Aquaba. [George calls the island Huarin, perhaps that really is one of its names along with Coral Island and Faroun. It was what is now called Pharaoh's Island, now in Israel. The lagoon lies in the south-western area of this popular tourist spot.]

Lawrence then left us just like any ordinary shipmate might. He probably went aboard the *Humber* as it provided night accommodation for the shore officers and our pilots.

George could not have had a better guide than the man who began his professional life as an archaeologist. The Bible refers to the place in 1 Kings 9:26:

King Solomon also built ships in Ezion-Geber, which is near Eilat in Edom, on the shores of the Red Sea.

This verse probably refers to an Iron Age port city on the same ground as modern Aqaba. Ezion-Geber was a city of Idunea, a biblical seaport in the area of modern Aqaba and Eilat, Israel's southernmost city. Eilat and Ezion-Geber were twin cities in Solomon's network of military border fortresses in the Negev.

And King Solomon made a navy of ships in Eziongeber, which is beside Eloth, on the shore of the Red Sea, in the land of Edom.

I Kings 9:26-29 (King James Version)

In his book *Lawrence and the Arabs* Graves tells of the visit made by Lawrence before the War.

…Woolley could not spare the three months that he was wanted for, so he and Lawrence went together for six weeks and divided the work between them. They got on well with the surveyor, Captain Newcombe, an Engineer officer who afterwards was in Arabia with Lawrence, and made important discoveries of ancient remains. They mapped out, not too seriously perhaps, the probable route of the Israelites' marches and found the place which may have been Kadesh Barnea where Moses struck the rock and water gushed out. They went as far as Petra and Maan in Arabia, places that figured importantly in Lawrence's campaign four years later. Their report appears in a book called *The Wilderness of Sin*, published in 1914 by the Palestine Exploration Fund. The survey could not be complete without certain bearings taken at the Red Sea port of Akaba, but the Turks had refused permission, for military reasons. Lawrence told Newcombe that he would go and look at Akaba. He got there without opposition and took what notes he wanted. Then he had a sudden desire to explore the ancient ruins on a little island called Faroun Island which lies a quarter of a mile from the coast. He asked permission to use the one boat that was on the beach. The Turks refused and a large party drew the boat up on the beach so that he could not possibly move it. That did not stop Lawrence. In the middle of the day when all Turkish soldiers go to sleep he made a raft out of three of his large camel water-tanks. These copper tanks hold eighteen gallons apiece and measure about three feet six inches by one foot three inches, and are nine inches deep; they make excellent rafts. The wind took him safely across and he inspected the ruins, but he had difficulty on the return journey. The water was full of sharks, too. The survey, I should be explained, was ordered by Kitchener for military purposes. But it was disguised as archaeology. The Palestine Exploration Fund got permission from the Turks for it and the task of Lawrence and Woolley was, they found on arrival, to provide the archaeological excuse for Newcombe's map-making activities.[46]

George continues:

It was about then that Lawrence had been active in preparing himself to visit Feisal again. What a setback he would have had if those two RFC officers and not made that spontaneous sudden decision to attack the Turkish cavalry. At the time, Major Bannatyne, our squadron commander, was over the front with a machine-gun doing his utmost in support of our troops. No time had to be lost to save the whole of Sinai army from another defeat. It surprised me then and it surprises me now why the RFC and the RAF hid the exploits of such men. They seem to have hidden the exploits of many more pilots who have passed into oblivion.

Nevertheless, the speed of that attack and the end surprised everyone when it came. The fact that our planes had been sent to work in Aquaba, that new matting hangars had been built suggested that the conflict would last much longer. We thought that X Flight was on its way to being built up to full squadron ready for a lengthier campaign.

War in Desert Over: Leave in Suez

George wrote:

> Although our hangars in Mudowwara were built in May 1918 they were never used after June. Then after a switch-over to a landing ground in Gueira, we built a hangar there which was intended to last longer than September because there was then no sign of an early finish to the war. Plans for an early finish were kept so secret that the end when it came was a surprise to us all. Suddenly in late September, we received orders to return quickly to our base at Aquaba.
>
> We lost the BE12 [that was] Junor's machine but ended up with our other nine machines that were flown over to Egypt. We were stripping down hangars a week later in Suez then before the end of October we received our first leave after having been out on the front line since 1915.

OCTOBER 1918

George continues:

> The war ended in the desert and some of us were able to get to Egypt, to Suez on about the 28 October on ten days' leave on the first holiday since my arrival in 1915. We stayed in the Royal Hotel, Cairo, for the whole ten days arriving back at Suez on 11 November 1918.
>
> During that time, Sergeant Ross and I travelled in a hired taxi from Cairo to Heliopolis to meet Porter who had almost died of thirst in the desert. He was there with a couple of our original team who had been posted there to help build up the maintenance workshops.

For George and his comrades that stay in the hotel in Cairo must have been like a release from bondage. He had lived a truly monastic life during those years he served with X Flight. Postulants to monastic life voluntarily accepted vows of poverty, chastity and obedience, George had them imposed upon him. The poverty: for much of the time he lived on bully beef and hard army biscuits, wore simple RFC clothing, slept rough and drew minimal pay. The chastity: he was unmarried and behaved himself as much out of necessity as wisdom. The obedience: that was essential in any branch of the armed services. Fortunately for the pilots of X Flight his obedience, like so many of his skilled colleagues, was more like religious devotion as he put his heart and soul into keeping the aircraft in safe working order!

George continues:

> We met Stokes [3326 Corporal T.R. Stokes joined C Flight on 2 June 1917], who was one of our party in El Wejh and had landed with us, the seven mechanics at Aquaba, to help in our support work with Lawrence's army. He had been posted to Egypt in May 1918. He arranged our meeting with Porter. We talked about old friends and events and arranged to spend an evening in our rooms at the Royal Hotel.

We dined sumptuously with champagne and finally relaxed in comfort in our sitting room for the evening, steadily working our way through Crown and Pilsener beers on ice. We gradually learnt the truth about Stafford and Porter's experiences.

Porter spoke, 'You know the conditions out there. Well! We had to make our way back with no compass and no road wheel tracks to guide us in the correct direction to the drome. Our radiator began to go on the boil but we had to try and save as much of the water as possible for ourselves. We were not getting any nearer to the drome because we had been travelling in circles until it became impossible to continue. We had to stop and hope that some relief would turn up. Among those hills we were probably invisible to our aircraft and we were too dazed to see an aircraft if it approached.

'On the second day without drinking water we were compelled to try and moisten our lips with urine for what little we could muster.' He became distressed to look back on his experience so we made him pause and relax a little with his beer, 'It's so good to enjoy a beer or any drink now!'

'We were in a really bad state later that second day. Then during the next day after a terrible night of suffering, old Stafford was starting to give in and prepare to pack it all in but I attempted to brace him up stick it out.

'He was getting very feverish and I must have been too because we were shouting and singing as I tried to buck Stafford up, "Don't forget your wife and kiddies!" The time was dragging on and still there were no signs of any human beings. As the sun became hotter than ever and our sufferings grew, we finally decided to use the gun on ourselves.'

Porter stopped talking for a while to regain his composure. 'But while still fighting against our decision, suddenly we saw the camel and the Arab. We could hardly speak let alone shout but we waved and tottered towards him. He spotted us and gave us water from his goat skin bottle.

'A grateful Stafford put his hand in his pocket and offered him some sovereigns but the Arab refused. We just expressed our gratitude. He too was pleased. The Arab threw his hands up heavenwards and called out, "Allah be praised!" helping us both onto his camel and got us to the beach.'

George added:

Those of us who were there in desert realised that it was a war altogether different from the wars on the Western Front where the suffering was much greater.

The conflict had come to an end and our flight was ordered to leave our camp at Gueira and move back to Aquaba with instructions to get out as quickly as possible.

THE OFFICIAL END OF X FLIGHT

When it came the end of X Flight arrived suddenly and unexpectedly. It was brought about not by enemy action, but by decisions in the Command structure.

118

The Flight and its work were to be kept secret and so it has been for over ninety years. Even the official documents concerning the end of X Flight and now held by the Public Records Office were marked 'Secret'.

One of those papers was from HQ, Middle East, to various Commanding Officers including the base Paymaster. The irony should be noted. Neither George, nor his companions in arms, ever received their back pay for service with X Flight. X Flight was so secret that the government forgot to pay any of the personnel.

That particular paper read:

> Orders have been issued for the withdrawal of 'X' Flight from AKABA to EGYPT, consequent on the termination of active operations in the AKABA area.
>
> The Flight Commander has been instructed to notify his shipping requirements to the commandant AKABA.
>
> All possible machines will be flown to SUEZ.
>
> The Flight will temporarily be located on SUEZ, AERODROME. Pending decision as to their future employment.
>
> Signed by Lt. Colonel R. Russell, S.O.1. (Air) 2-10-1918

A follow-up memo from HQ Training dated 6 October 1918 said that officers may be granted leave but must be ready to return on twenty-four hours' notice. Another dated the next day refers, not to X Flight but to the 'AKABA FLIGHT'. One wonders if that was a deliberate attempt to write the Flight out of the history books.

A further letter marked 'URGENT SECRET', from 32nd Training Wing to No. 58 Training Squadron dated 12 October 1918, said:

> Lts. Murphy and Hawley, Pilot and Observer respectively of the Bristol Fighter have been retained in CAIRO under instructions from G.O.C., Middle East.
>
> The remaining Pilots will fly their Machines to No. 5 Fighting School. Training, Heliopolis, No. Fighting School and this Office to be advised time of departure.
>
> The Air mechanics will proceed to No. 5 Fighting School by first train on the morning of the 14th instant.

Another letter marked 'SECRET' of the same date issued by Headquarters of the Training Brigade, Royal Air Force, Middle East, gave instructions for the:

> …recall of X Flight from leave and arrange to move this unit to be attached to No. 5 Fighting School, 38th Training Wing. As soon as possible.
>
> 1 Bristol Fighter
>
> 1 B.E.2.E
>
> 2 B.E.12s
>
> Remainder by rail.

All arrangements for the move will be made under your orders and you will give 24 hours notice by telegram to these Headquarters, stating the time of arrival of the personnel.

The machines will be sent off as soon as the Pilots report from leave.

Except for the Bristol Fighters, recent additions, the aeroplanes were the old faithful work horses of X Flight.

SECRET COPY ORDER NO. 15 HQ ROYAL AIR FORCE, MIDDLE EAST

'X' Flight disembarked at SUEZ from AKABA on the 20th instant.

The Flight will be re-organised as a four Aeroplane Flight, (2 BE.12s) 2 B.E. 2Es.) [sic], and will proceed to HAIFA for antisubmarine duty under the orders of the Senior Naval officer, HAIFA.

While reorganising at SUEZ the personnel of the flight will be attached for administration, rations and discipline to the Training Brigade, but the Flight Commander will communicate directly with H.Q., R.A.F., Middle East, on the subject of equipment.

The move of the Flight from SUEZ to HAIFA will be arranged by H.Q., R.A.F., Middle East.

On arrival at HAIFA the flight will be attached to Palestine Brigade for administration, rations and discipline, and will operate under the orders of the Senior Naval officer, HAIFA.

Captain V.D. Siddons will report himself on Wednesday, the 23rd instant, to the Officer Commanding, 'XX' Anti-Submarine Flight, Abukir, and will be temporarily attached to that Flight for the purpose of familiarising himself with methods of Anti-Submarine work and co-operation with the navy for a maximum of seven days.

He will, as soon as he is in a position to do so, submit to H.Q., R.A.F., Middle East, detailed suggestions for the establishment including all transport and stores.

The aeroplane will fly to HAIFA via Kantara and Ramleh.

(Sgd) M.N. Russell Lieutenant-Colonel, S.O.I. (Air), Royal Air Force, Middle East. H.Q. Cairo. 21/10/18

T.B.No.C/1559, 21/10/18 M.E.No.GS.501/F, 21/10/18

George tells it as it was for the men of X Flight as their duties came to an end.

We stripped down all the equipment and sailed for Suez in November 1918. It was the case of keeping our exploits in support of the Arab revolt dark. At El Wejh as far as we were concerned our war was being won by Lawrence and his army although we knew little of his plans. Secrecy had been essential throughout to ensure surprise when Lawrence attacked. We did our bit working at the drome.

We had been engaged in it and on the way we celebrated at Aquaba by holding a conference about Billy the Goat, one of two which Furness-Williams had bought from a lone Arab woman who had escaped the attention of the Turks. One night on Decie mudflat, in January 1918, when sitting at our camp fire, Furness-Williams went for a run out to the hills in our Crossley. While out there, he bought the young kids. We killed one and put it in the cooking pot as a change from our daily ration of bully beef and biscuits. We kept the one at Aquaba as a mascot.

On the day before we finally packed up, we decided to cook him. One of transport drivers, Davies [3064 X Flight RFC and RAF attached Hedjaz Wing 1916/18], who had been a London cook killed cleaned and chopped him up making it the best meal we ever had in Arabia. The goat had been nine months older but the fattest animal in the whole of Arabia.

We also had two pet pups which had been found in the desert. Our naval commander allowed us to take them away with us to Egypt.

The four original machines which we never expected to survive a submarine attack made upon our ship in the Med on the way out actually went on to serve right through the Middle East and Arabian war. They were powered by 90 horsepower eight cylinder engines and bearing in mind they worked in temperatures of about 110 degrees, never once did they fail us. They had received our expert attention throughout and we resent the sneering remarks that the machines were fastened with wire and bits of string. The only machine we ever lost was the BE12 and that was in combat in the last few days of the final push. It was Junor's aircraft but it really was suicidal for him to have to fly into the Palestine front where enemy opposition was very strong.

On October 31 1918 Turkey surrendered.

11 NOVEMBER 1918

George continues:

It was exactly the 11th of November 1918, when after arriving back in Suez, for about fifteen minutes along the railway run to Suez we were cheered by the natives of Egypt as we passed them on the way to our destination. We were surprised about the extraordinary excitement of the people, we then learnt that the Germans had packed in! The same excitement filled our drome. Officers and other ranks downed tools and began a night of celebration.

Lawrence's victory had gone as planned and Germany had collapsed a few weeks later. We fell into bored inactivity having nothing to do except walking up and down in the vicinity of our CO's marquee waiting for further in instructions. I received a letter from home on the 12th November 1918 saying that my younger brother Jim was expected home after being a prisoner of war in Germany for nearly two years.

He had volunteered at seventeen and half years of age, serving in France with the Connaught Rangers. There he contracted trench fever and after a spell at home recovering, he returned to the Western Front and took part in fighting on the Somme. While taking part in a night raid, all but he in the raiding party were killed, but he suffered from a bullet wound in the chest and was taken prisoner at Givenchy. After recovering from his wounds, presumably, he was finally put to work in the mines.

The last letter I wrote to him, when I was at Aquaba, may have been forwarded to the POW camp in Germany in June 1918. In a letter to my father Jim said he felt he could not stand it much longer in the prison camp. My letter was intended to buck him up as tactfully as I could asking him to bear up because the war would be over in a few months. I doubt that he received it though.

In reply to my Dad's letter, I wrote telling him that I might not get home for Christmas but he could tell Jim to have a good time and have a glass of wine for me.

WAITING TO EMBARK FOR HOME

George continues:

The next day I had received a visit from Colonel Grant Dalton from Cairo headquarters. As a pilot, he had served in Suez defending the canal but he received a bullet in the leg. The wound resulted in an amputation of one leg making him unfit to continue air duties. I had no idea where he had continued with the RFC until he sent a junior officer to see me as I was standing near our camp. A young officer approached me and asked if I was Sergeant Hynes. On replying that I was, the officer said, 'Colonel Grant Dalton sends his compliments. I have to tell you that he will be over to see you and Corporal New.' I brought Corporal New over at once.

Colonel Grant Dalton arrived and shook hands with us and told us how delighted he was to see us. He asked me if I had been home since I came out to Egypt.

I replied that I had not been home during that time. 'Hynes you are classified as the engineering expert in the Middle East. Your record on aircraft maintenance is wonderful considering the machines you had and all the flying hours they had to do with no replacements. I have a new job for you. You will take over at Shalluffa and you will be promoted so I will send for you in three weeks time. Go and get some leave in the meantime.' He wished me well and left by air for Cairo.

I was never been approached by Captain Siddons in that matter and was about to request some leave to break the monotony, when I received word from my father that Jim had been reported as having passed away two days before Armistice Day. The news had come as a severe shock to him as he had only just returned from the city [Liverpool] to obtain some wine to brace Jim up and help to regain his strength after his bad time as a prisoner of war.

On my way to Captain Siddons' tent, I felt it my duty to apply for home leave yet at the same time I did not want to disappoint Colonel Grant Dalton or to let anyone down. However I put in my request and was granted leave and given a travel warrant. I was so upset that I cannot remember how I spent that Christmas Day in 1918.

A month or two later, George's younger brother, Richard, after fighting in the trenches, served with the occupation troops in Germany. One evening, when out walking across a bridge over a river and feeling upset about his brother's death in the POW camp, he punched every German male he met and threw them into the river!

George saw Lawrence for the last time.

That outing, to the island, was last time I saw Lawrence. A couple of weeks later, with our equipment stored aboard ship, and our aircraft flown to Egypt, we set steam for Cairo. We received some of our pay and that enabled us to spend ten days' leave there.

GEORGE LEAVES THE MIDDLE EAST

George recalls:

That was largely due to the fact that I had to wait for three weeks in the embarkation station at Portslade along with thousands of other troops and much unrest due to a Whitehall order that all coal miners were to be sent home first.

I kept to my camp like a lost sheep without being able to draw any of my back pay. Troops were getting out of hand to prevent the miners, needed to get our mines back into production, from boarding ships ahead of them. Those who had seen long periods of service especially the wounded who had lost arms and legs but had been kept so long in Egypt. They had to wait during the conflict because of the enemy submarine activity in the Med. They were now very angry.

The day arrived when I was called to embark and joined a party of five RAF who were marched off to another dock where the sheds were filled with men of every British Regiment. We were all loaded with kit, and like myself, a few oriental souvenirs tucked away in our two kit bags.

Our party was lined up to board the SS *California* joining the long lines of troops climbing the ship's gangways. It took two hours before we set foot on deck after getting soaked on the quayside when torrents of rain poured down on us for over an hour. The rain even got into our kit bags!

That was the first time in the Middle East that I experienced a soaking. There seemed to be no such thing as rainfall in Arabia. There it would have been thought of as golden rain falling on wide open sun dried sands and hills where the green scrub grew only about one sixteenth of an inch a year.

Those green scrubs gave off a lovely fragrance at dawn like the smell of lime juice but as the sun rose higher our nostrils were robbed of those early morning fragrances. Very early morning in the desert filled us with feelings of how good it was to be alive. At those times many an Arab could be seen urging his horse into energetic dashes around and over the sand hills and those green tufts of scrub, about twelve to eighteen inches high.

On board the crowded ship, I had plenty of time to reflect upon the pleasures of the Arabian wastes as I sat saturated to the skin on or under a table along with other service men huddled together at night on floors without bedding to ease aching limbs. We had no means of drying our clothes during the three days and nights on board ship as we sailed to Taranto in Italy with the sight of Vesuvius across the bay.

Taranto is an important commercial port and coastal city in Puglia, Italy. There, on 11 November 1940, twenty-one British Swordfish armed with torpedoes managed to cripple the Italian Fleet. Today it is the main Italian naval base and a one-time seaplane school. The first British troop train left Cherbourg for Taranto in June 1917. The rolling stock was provided by the British and the French operated the system to their border whence the Italians took over running the trains with British coal. The Royal Engineers provided the transit camps at both ends of the line which was about 1,100 miles in length and along which trains travelled at an average speed of 67 miles a day!

George continues:

> I did have time to do some thinking about Lieutenant General Salmond, Senior Commander of the Royal Flying Corps. In him, we had the best type of commander, one who did not sit on his bottom wrapped in a cloak of professional self-importance. He was a fighter who took to the air himself in major battles during our Sinai operations to see for himself how operations were progressing.
>
> Requests had been made from England that those mechanics due for promotion should be sent home to help in the expansion of the RFC as soon as word had been received that the Turks had been defeated on the canal. Geoffrey Salmond hung on to his mechanics because his men had been acclimatised. He could not spare them as our squadron was supplying his skilful craftsmen and organising the expansion that was required in the Middle East. Salmond held on to the early skilled volunteers who had been received in Farnborough in 1914. He said that he could not allow us to take our wings as the mechanics were more valuable in the care of his aircraft than in flying them.

Although skilled craftsmen were often overlooked for promotion because of the importance of their jobs [they] did not become less efficient or careless in their work because they knew they just had to keep their aircraft in tip top condition for the sake of the pilots who flew them. They took pride in their aircraft.

A TERRIBLE JOURNEY FROM ITALY TO CHERBOURG

George continues:

Taranto, Italy, was not a pleasant picture, making me feel I would never want to go there again. I decided I did not want to spend any time in Italy during the winter. We had arrived in a miserable snowed up country from equatorial hot atmosphere in clothes that were still damp. There was nowhere in Taranto where we could dry them nor anywhere where we could get cash to buy some warm drinks.

We were housed [in] prefabricated, iron half-cylindrical huts and in my own case, wearing boots with soles that were almost worn through after four years use. [The huts referred to would have been Nissen huts invented in 1916 by Major Peter Norman Nissen of the 29th Company Royal Engineers.] My feet were wet the whole time.

We then travelled in railway wagons rather like meat vans which took ten days to travel from Taranto to Cherbourg. We travelled in a far from pleasant state of mind, as our discomforts were aggravated by snowfalls on the railway tracks. Men were badly smitten by the cold which was hardly eased by occasional cups of weak tea at some railway stops with hardly more encouragement than 'On your way, pals!' and doses of pills to help us in our feverish conditions.

There were a few who died on that journey. I lost my voice, suffered from a sore throat and rebelled over the poor treatment we received at Cherbourg after a long march uphill to the camp.

During that journey through Italy it was depressing to see Italian soldiers on guard duties looking the worse for wear and war in badly shod boots at railway crossings. At many crossings, young girls and women begged for food offering bottles of wine for cheese or bully beef. Our infantry pals seemed to have cash and [were] able to pay for a loaf of bread and a bottle of wine. Some gave their own bully beef away. I was too sick myself to eat anything so I threw my tins to a youngster as there was great poverty in abundance. Even the dogs in the snowed up villages could be heard howling for food. Italy was in a bad way. I had no hesitation in throwing them my tin of bully.

Lawrence must have known how uncomfortable the Taranto/Cherbourg route could be because although usually indifferent to rank he actually asked to be made a full colonel to secure himself a berth on the staff train which accepted only full colonels and above! He called it his 'Taranto rank'.[47]

George continues:

> In Cherbourg, I insisted upon seeing the medical officer at eight o'clock at night as I had been doped with quinine for ten days and had lost my voice. I was, in fact, examined with another Tommy of about my own age and taken to Thorville Chateau and for the first time in years put into a lovely clean bed. Unfortunately, Shaughnessy, poor kid, who was also placed there, was carried out dead the next morning.

There are several chateaux in or near Cherbourg. Chateau des Ravales seems closest to the harbour.

George continues:

> I was cared for by an elderly nurse and attended by an army doctor about five days after my arrival. The doctor advised me that I could be released if I was going home but if not, I was to stay for three weeks in hospital and I was allowed out for a couple of days.
>
> When the time came, my nurse told me that I could go back to Blighty and I should change out of hospital clothes in a closet. However when I went to put on my Royal Flying Corps uniform, I discovered that my grey backed shirt was full of lice.
>
> As it was my first time ever in hospital, being cared for by a 'Lady with the Lamp'. I was very embarrassed to discover the lice and far too ashamed to tell her, so I stole the hospital pyjamas and put them on. Wearing them as I moved into a camp, to the Warrant Officers' hut to stay until I was shipped to England.
>
> I immediately put my shirt into a pail of water, put soft soap in the pail, placed it on a coke stove and sat near it to keep warm and waiting for the vermin to be destroyed. I wrung the water out, put my shirt on a line near the stove to dry. Then with my task completed I would have a clean shirt to wear on my way to Blighty.
>
> The shirt had only been about half an hour on the line, when the W.O. told me to get my kit, and to take charge of a party of soldiers discharged from the hospital, and march them to the docks to board a cross Channel boat that was to leave at midnight.
>
> I rebelled again and refused to walk them with our kits. Instead I demanded a motor truck to carry us there. It was granted. On board ship an American cross channel tramp, and packed like cattle, many were sea sick, poor blighters, even after going through a gruelling in those muddy trenches in France.

January 1919

George recalls:

> On my way home, in January 1919, I landed in Southampton to be faced with a railway strike. The boys from the prison camps and all returning soldiers were hoping to board trains to take them to the depots for overseas leave and demob but they then had to endure the hardship of walking up and down on the station platforms until the next day.

AUSSIE VETERAN

George continues:

> Arriving next morning about six o'clock, no rations or cash we were sent off to the railway station carrying kit bags and packs. A Dinkum shouted to me:
> 'Hello, buddy!'
> I turned to him and replied, 'Hello, pal!' 'Don't you remember me?'
> 'I am afraid I don't. You have the advantage.'
> 'I was in the Patrol that was guarding your party on Salek Zowaid at the Battle of Rafa when you landed there covering our troops.'

That would have been on 9 January 1917. After a victory at Romani on 4 August 1916, British forces took the offensive in the Sinai. In December, the same year, ANZAC forces reached El Arish in the eastern Sinai and captured the garrison at Magdhaba. Then in January 1917, the Battle of Rafa took place at the outpost of Rafa (Rafah) on the border between the Egyptian Sinai and Palestine up until then a part of the Ottoman Empire. Ottoman forces were driven out of the Sinai.

George continues:

> I answered him, 'As you know we were all very occupied but I do remember our little chat. You have a good memory. What are you doing here?'
> 'I have been given a few months leave to visit my uncle and aunt in Shrewsbury. I have never met them but was determined to see them before going back to Australia.'
> I told him I was pleased to meet him and he said, 'Yes, you were lucky that evening when you and your pilot (Major Bannatyne) were the last to take off to return to your base, the Turkish aircraft had come over to try and demolish your machines, dropped a stick of bombs just as you were about to leave the ground, and fortunately for me, I was making a billy can of tea behind a sand dune when some of his bombs killed my horse on the other side of the dune, otherwise I would have got it also.'
> 'Yes, my pal, Pendron had told me about that when he got back with his camels that had brought up our petrol supplies and bombs and told us he

127

dropped under a camel's belly. The enemy machine had missed its real target as we were in the air and, as the major in command, my pilot saw them all off. We joined up in the rear as he told me that our day's operation was very successful, and that the two remaining redoubts would be taken by your boys at about two o'clock in the morning.'

The Australian said, 'Well it's good to be here, so what about breakfast?'

I replied, 'Come on, we will find a place somewhere in the dock area but I am sorry I can't treat you it as I am broke having not received any pay since I left Suez. I expected an officer at the docks to help us out, and all I have is my railway ticket for Farnborough.'

'I'm alright. Come on. We are buddies in distress and you do the ordering.'

We both trudged along to the nearest eating house. It was the usual cocoa rooms that all dock areas have. Walking up to the counter I placed my order.

'Two bacon and eggs, please!'

The proprietor replied, 'Bacon and eggs! There has been a war on!'

I replied, 'So I believe! I heard that when we were out there for three years living on bully beef! Well what have you for a snack?'

'Only salt fish.'

'Give us two plates of salt fish then with two large cups of tea and some bread and marg. And give us the tea now, hot!'

We received our eats and settled down to breakfast, and conversing as soldiers do. After my friend had eaten his fish, he said, 'I have never tasted this before. It's good. I'll have another one.' And so I went over for another and two more 'doorsteps' [thick slices of bread].

After eating breakfast, I prepared to have a smoke for I had not enjoyed one since I went into hospital and I opened one of my two kit bags pulling out a few packets of cigarettes. I opened one offering my buddy one and lit up to sit back for a little to relax and handed the packets over to my chum.

'Let me pay my respects to you as it is a pleasure to give them to you.'

'I don't want to rob you of them, you may need them as I was told there is a railway strike on and God knows when we get to our destinations.'

'Take them. I have plenty more in my bag and they are stolen during my trip through from Taranto.'

I told him that it happened when our train arrived in French territory and pulled up for the night in a siding. Some of the other troops had spotted a catering tent and had gone over to try and get some hot drinks and eats but they were barred from entering it for it was a Yankee canteen and refused to allow our chaps permission to enter.

During the early hours of the morning, it must have been about three o'clock, a couple had pushed their heads inside our truck. 'Come on boys, and help yourself to biscuits, chocolate, and cigs and a bottle of wine to warm you!'

Although we were sleeping in our uniforms, with only two army blankets to keep us warm, we jumped out into the cold and clambered aboard the goods train that had pulled up alongside us.

The British ants had been busy when we joined them and about three cases were put in our truck and a couple of bottles of wine and stored in the corner with a couple having to sleep on the top of the cases. We enjoyed some wine but I left my eats due to having a very sore throat but took my share of the swag in cigs and some small packets of biscuits.

Well my Australian buddy enjoyed a good laugh, and said he was enjoying his cig, and so was I, for it was the first for several weeks.

I questioned him about the strike as he had to go to a different station to mine, and we parted, but he was the first friend in Blighty [I was] to meet but one I would never have expected to meet in England. I always think of him that some time I may be able to repay that comradeship if not to him, but [for it] to be recorded and repay him for his generosity in his homeland of Australia, for as he was leaving me he shook hands and pressed two half crowns into my hand.

'This will help you until you get to your destination.'

So we parted but really we could never have kept up that friendship. It became one of those memories that we treasure; a memory of that spirit of comradeship linking us with the Imperial volunteers. The ones who jumped to it when Britain had to face those days in what we thought was a War to end Wars.

I was bundled on to a train to take me to a receiving station in Blandford but instead I was dropped off at lonely country stations on the way. Three days later after cold wintry nights I eventually arrived at my destination, Blandford, at about nine o'clock at night.

During the year 1918, Blandford changed from being the depot for the Royal Naval Division to an 'Intake Camp' for the RFC undergoing transformation as the RAF. A branch railway line took materials and personnel to the camp. By the end of 1919, the camp was closed and the camp's railway line was removed. By the end of 1920, the site had been cleared.

George continues:

Fortunately a Flight Sergeant received me and he, hearing I was from the Middle East, was anxious to know if I had met his brother out there. In fact, I had, but had to tell him that the man had died. His brother had been an officer's servant and was one of three who had run out of their tent when an enemy machine had dropped some bombs. They were killed when a bomb dropped just in front of them.

When dinner was finished in the mess, my new friend treated me to a large whisky and I was able to get a good night's sleep.

129

Next morning I reported with the many new arrivals to be quickly fitted out with the new RAF uniform and clean, all round kit. We then had our medical examinations, there in that camp which accommodated about one hundred and fifty men from all war areas. Among them were former prisoners of war, some with missing arms and legs lying on low trestle and board beds about ten inches off the floor.

I fondly remember the comfort of soft sandy beds on ground sheets in the desert where one could scoop sand out to bring greater comfort for the body. I heard stories about Cut Throat Wood where soldiers with leg amputations had got fed up waiting for a posting home [and] had ended their misery.

I enjoyed being on advanced operations, although we had less food and comforts than those at the base it gave one the pleasure of getting stuck into the work, enjoy it, and face the hardship and at the same time be free to put all one's efforts into it. We could enjoy the loneliness of the open tracts of territory and the beauty of the hills. Our conditions were more pleasant than those of our troops in France during those winter months.

That first night after my arrival, I decided to go into the mess, a shanty of a place, to meet some of the boys and seek a little comfort. I sat in a wicker armchair near the only heating, a coke burning stove. We drank a beer or two discussing our experiences. I was most interested in the prisoners of war who had been shot down or taken during the enemy advances.

While there, we were approached by an NCO who had left a group who seemed to be 'well loaded' at the bar, about twenty members of the Women's Royal Air Force, a couple of them sitting on a bar counter. The NCO met us with, 'Well chaps what about making room for our lady friends?'

One bold sitter said, 'I am afraid you are unlucky this time, mate. We have just come from a very warm climate where we didn't enjoy the comforts of you chaps.'

The senior NCO got a little shirty. Another sitter, missing an arm, said, 'Your lady friends seem pretty warm. I am afraid that they seem to be well oiled and very comfortable as is, so take a walk and ease down on your stride!' and we all agreed.

The next morning it was 'fall in and follow the crowd' into a large hut to report for travel warrants and pay. I drew twenty pounds from my back pay. By three o' clock I was on my way, getting into Liverpool at six the following morning where my first task was to get a decent breakfast before going home.

I stepped out into Lime Street and entered the underground café just outside and ordered ham and eggs and a cup of tea and after hearing of the shortage of supplies, I was surprised to be supplied with both.

I sat down, enjoyed my breakfast and looked at the bulky surroundings and somehow I felt that there was more beauty in the hills and sands of

Arabia. Having completed my smoke, I boarded the tram for home. I arrived there just as my dad was going to work to the mill across the road where he was works manager. My mother and he and told me what little they knew about my brother's death. The shock was particularly severe because they had been expecting him home quite soon.

My father had received a letter from the German government saying that they were sorry to have to say that Jim had passed away. The news arrived on the day that Dad had returned from the city with a few bottles of wine to brace Jim up.

He wrote to Lloyd George for some confirmation but was told that they could not help at that time and my dad never forgot it. He then replied to [the] German government. A reply came from the padre who had attended Jim before he passed away and saw him buried, giving particulars of the burial place.

It was a blow to me and I became very angry at those who had brought the war on. I felt sorry for all who had sacrificed their lives. All I then wanted to do was to break free from military discipline and return to living a life of my own.

The news of the death of James Edward Hynes arrived as a great blow to the whole family. It was such a pity, occurring as it did in the last week of the Great War. George's oldest brother John had served through the whole conflict on the Western Front and a younger brother, Richard, was still serving there.

There are several intriguing comments made by George in his memoirs about inaccuracies in various accounts about Lawrence's wartime activities. George wrote:

I repeat that much information about those operations, if permitted could have been obtained from Salmond, Williams, Stent, Siddons, Borton and others; but reading that only two aircraft were used by 'X' Flight gives me the opinion that the Air Ministry had been compelled to dodge the true story, except for the lack of reports of air activity between Cairo and Whitehall.

Speedily breaking up the Special Duty Flight, had to do with a deliberate attempt to forget that it ever existed. Very few people in Britain had known that such a campaign had ever taken place. Lowell Thomas was the first person to release the shackles of diplomatic secrecy of the otherwise unknown Lawrence of Arabia, when he displayed the actual film of those operations from January 1918 from Aquaba to the entry of Feisal and Lawrence in Damascus.

From January 1918, the Royal Flying Corps, special duty flight, had been made up of six pilots with ten aircraft built up from four bomber machines and four pilots in October 1917.

In support there was an armoured car section, five cars and about thirty five personnel, four officers, two of them with the machine gun section.

Officers and men of the Royal Army Ordnance Corps, Major Marshall and Captain Ramsey, a small base staff of Royal Army Medical Corps and Royal Army Service Corps dealing with supplies. Colonel Joyce was Camp Commandant at Aquaba except when he went forward with the troops on the final drive.

I can safely state that the total number of officers and ranks in Aquaba, was no more than 110 men in base duties including our flight and in close contact with the Arabs until the last month of the drive from Guerra to Damascus then joined by officers from Allenby's staff.

In fact we [X Flight] were so isolated in Arabia, that I lost over forty pounds of back pay and the extra shilling per day hardship allowance due to the fact that it was not recorded in the Pay Office in England. After many requests to the Paymaster of the R.A.F., my legal claims were just ignored.

Forty pounds in 1920 had the same purchasing power of at least £1,250 today, probably more. His hardship allowance could have amounted to about the same sum.

1932

GEORGE WRITES TO LAWRENCE

By the time George was corresponding with Lawrence in the mid-1930s the country of Transjordan in which they had spent their years of war was a Mandate of Great Britain, ruled by the Emir Abdullah, son of King Hussein, and brother of King Feisal of Iraq.

George married Hannah Dulson, who was his fiancée when he went out to serve in Arabia. Their children were: George, a child James who died at age two, Vincent, Joan, Ellen and Thomas Hynes. He continued work as an engineer and inventor patenting, among other things, an Internal Combustion Gas Turbine, a car safety belt and an instant locking device for fireguards. Unfortunately he did not have the resources to follow up most of them but he did make and sell the fireguard security locks.

In 1932, George wrote to Lawrence (Aircraftsman Shaw) summarising his personal history since 1919. A son, also called George, was born in 1920 and other children followed hence the '…forging ahead in family' reference in Lawrence's letter.

338171 A/c Shaw
R.A.F.
Mount Batten
Plymouth.
25.x.32

Dear Hynes

Congratulations on George. I hope he and Mrs. Hynes are flourishing. You are forging ahead in family!

I'm back in my proper place now, the motor boats all finished and running strongly. To be in camp again is like a rest cure. The hours seem so short. Just at the moment my job is to pull to bits a seized up motor boat engine. It is rather a puzzle, everything being rusted solid.

Akaba had the better climate, anyway. Engines didn't rust solid in a week! Parts of our war were not so bad, I suppose, though personally I hated it.

You shall have that photo when I come across something possible: but I won't go to a photographer and be taken. There are copies of some artists' drawings that I need to have. One of those when I lay my hands on them again. No papers in camp!

Yours truly, TE Shaw

RAF Mount Batten began as a seaplane base during the First World War. The Royal Navy Air Service Station became RAF Cattewater in 1918, re-opening on 1 October 1928 as RAF Mount Batten. It was located on a peninsula in Plymouth Sound. The next year Lawrence had moved to Southampton.

13 Birmingham St.
Southampton

21.xii.33

Dear Hynes

Still there? Probably not. I'm in Southampton for the moment, building boats for the R.A.F. My proper station is at Felixstowe. Where I expect to be for the next fourteen months. After that I get my lounge suit and have to look after myself.

I hope your affairs are well. This has been a rotten year for everybody. Let's hope 1934 is a bit more prosperous. I'm afraid it won't be as fine a summer, though. It was like the East, down here: week after week of sunshine and warmth. Lovely.

Best wishes for 1934

Yours
T.E. Shaw

The original two letters, given here, are now held in the Lawrence collection of the Houghton Library, University of Harvard.

Lawrence, T.E. Shaw, was killed on 14 May 1935 travelling at very high speed on his motorcycle on a Dorset road. Of the funeral George said:

> When he died, I sent a piece of rush-grass that I'd brought back from Akaba to his brother, A.W. Lawrence, who wrote to tell me that it had been placed in the coffin with Lawrence's body and buried with him.[48]

1939

GEORGE REJOINS THE RAF

One fascinating fact is that after George had rejoined the RAF during the Second World War (his son George also joined), he discovered that he was working on the same boats that had kept Lawrence busy some eight years earlier.

> One day during my overhauling duties, the young orderly room clerk at our workshop on the prom drew my attention to a Log Book where Lawrence was shown as the mechanic who carried out the maintenance. One was numbered 244, the one which had the seized up engine. A co-incidence I never thought possible.

In 1938, George, the eldest son, then eighteen and an apprentice motor engineer, joined the Auxiliary Air Force. His other son also wanted to join. On first application, all were accepted for service as was George himself but Group Command at first rejected George senior on the grounds that he was then forty-three years old. Despite that first rejection, on the day war broke out George was back in uniform in his war substantive rank of Sergeant! Within a few weeks he was posted to RAF Appledore, then a GCI and VEB Station, to work on boats. One of his first tasks was to install two 100 hp engines into a power boat in the Harris shipyard on the edge of the River Torridge, Appledore. His ingenuity and experience as both a marine and air mechanic served both him and the RAF well during that second conflict.

George's younger brother, Richard, who had served with the infantry on the Western Front in World War One, also rejoined, this time in the RAF for the duration of World War Two. By that time, their eldest brother, John, who had ended the War as a Warrant Officer Musketry Instructor at Bisley, had eventually died from the effects of a gassing he had suffered on the Western Front but his son, John, also joined the RAF.

NOTES

1 *Flight*, 18 January 1934.

2 Deramore, Lord et alia, *Winged Promises*, 1996, p.8.

3 Ibid, p.11.

4 Lawrence, T. E., *Seven Pillars of Wisdom*, Cape, 1973, Chapter LX.

5 *Flight*, 18 January 1934.

6 *Australian Flying Corps* on the internet.

7 Daddis, *Armageddon Lost*, citing Slater in *My Warrior Son*; *Barton Family*, p.25.

8 *London Gazette* – 27 March 1915.

9 *The Hejaz Narative* – the exploits of C Flight 14 Squadron RFC on the internet.

10 *Roger's Study; the Hejaz 1916* – Nominal roll of known participants on the internet.

11 *Winged Promises*, p.8.

12 Henderson, T., Captain, *The Exploits of 'C' Flight 14 Squadron RFC*, brought up to date by Roger Bragger.

13 Ibid.

14 Graves, Robert, *Lawrence and the Arabs*, Cape, 1927, p.209.

15 http://www.imagists.org/aldington/biography.html.

16 Graves, p.292.

17 Graves, p.89.

18 Lawrence, T.E., *Seven Pillars of Wisdom*, Cape, 1973, Chapter LVII, p.332.

19 Henderson, Salisbury, Christmas, 1917 as quoted in *The Hejaz Expedition 1916/17*.

20 Graves, appendix.

21 Lawrence, T.E., *Revolt in the Desert*, London, Flio Society, 1986 p.242.

22 *Flight*, 18 January 1934, No. 14 (Bomber) Squadron, Anon.

23 *Flight*, 18 January 1934.

24 Rudoe, Barbara, *The Life and Times of Frank Thornton Birkinshaw*, newly published work by his daughter.

25 *Australian Military History: An overview*, on the internet.

26 *Muscat Harbour*, March 2007, on the internet.

27 Rudoe, Barbara, *The Life and Times of Frank Thornton Birkinshaw*, by his daughter.

28 *RAF Flying Units in the South Midlands,* on the internet.

29 Raw-Rees, Owain, *The Order of Al Nahda of the Kingdom of Hijaz*, on the internet.

30 *Flight*, 18 January 1934. p.50.

31 Graves, p.11.

32 Adlington, Richard, *Lawrence of Arabia: A Biographical Enquiry*, Glasgow, 1955.

33 *Liverpool Echo and Evening Post*, 28 February 1963.

34 Ibid.

35 The *London Gazette*, 2 July 1915, War Office, 3 July 1915.

36 *Australin Flying Corps*, on the internet.

37 Lawrence, T. E., *Seven Pillars of Wisdom*, Book Seven, Chapter LXXXIV, p.478.

38 Lawrence, T. E., 'The Occupation of Akaba', *Arab Bulletin* No. 59.

39 Lawrence, T. E., *Seven Pillars of Wisdom*, 1973, Book Seven, Chapter XCIX.

40 Lawrence, T. E., *Seven Pillars of Wisdom*, 1973, Book Nine, Chapter CI.

41 Ibid.

42 *Australian Flying Corps*, on the internet.

43 Lawrence, T.E., *Seven Pillars of Wisdom*, Cape, London,1973, p.616

44 Lowell Thomas *With Lawrence in Arabia*, Collier.

45 *Australian Flying Corps*, on the internet.

46 Graves, pp.39, 40.

47 Graves, p.291.

48 *Liverpool Echo and Evening Post*, Thursday 28 February 1963.

Bibliography

Adlington, Richard, *Lawrence of Arabia: A Biographical Enquiry*, Glasgow, 1955

Deramore, Lord, Wing Commander E. Donovan, Dr V. Orange, Air Vice Marshal Stapleton, D.C., *Winged Promises; A History of No. 14 Squadron, RAF, 1915–1945*, 1996

Graves, Robert, *Lawrence and the Arabs*, Cape, 1927

Harvard University, Houghton Library Manuscripts, MS Eng 1252 Lawrence, T.E. (Thomas Edward), 1881–1935. Papers: 2 A.L.s. to George S. Hynes; Lawrence, Arnold Walter, 1900-A.L.s. to George S. Hynes; Cloud's Hill, 5 Jun 1935; (368) Hynes, George S. My Synopsis of T.E. Lawrence. A.M.S.; Liverpool. 10 Sep 1961 [n.d.]. 23s (23p)

Hynes, George, *Memoirs*, 1961, held by his daughter, Ellen Gannicott

Lawrence, T. E., *Seven Pillars of Wisdom*, Cape, 1973

Lawrence, T. E., *Revolt in the Desert*, London, Folio Society, 1986

Liverpool Echo and Evening Post, 28 February 1963

National Archives Public Record Office: AIR 1/477/15/312/230 X FLIGHT, AIR 1/2054/204/409/21 X FLIGHT

Rudoe, Barbara, *The Life and Times of Frank Thornton Birkinshaw*, newly published work by his daughter

INTERNET SOURCES

1 Squadron Australian Flying Corps, on the internet

Australian Military History: an overview, on the internet

Bragger, Roger & Wright, Peter, Lawrence's Air Force in the *Cross and Cockade*, Summer, 2003 on the internet. (My thanks to Cross and Cockade International for allowing the reproduction of a comment used in the Preface.)

Flight, 18 January 1934

Henderson, T., Captain, *The Hejaz Expedition, 1916–17* on the internet

London Gazette, 2 July 1915, War Office, 3 July 1915

LAWRENCE'S AIR FORCE

Captain Thomas Henderson's album, Lawrence's Air Force was C Flight of 14 Squadron, Royal Flying Corps that had been sent to the Hejaz at Captain Lawrence's request to assist in the Arab Revolt.

Thanks to Cross and Cockade International for allowing the reproduction of this article taken from their journal.

Index